Workplace Vocabulary

OrangeBooks Publication

Smriti Nagar, Bhilai, Chhattisgarh - 490020

Website: **www.orangebooks.in**

© Copyright, 2023, Author

First Edition, 2023

TALK LIKE A PRO: ESSENTIAL ENGLISH WORKPLACE VOCABULARY FOR SUCCESS

Empower Your Verbal Arsenal and Conquer the Corporate World

RAVIKIRAN REDDY

OrangeBooks Publication

www.orangebooks.in

PREFACE

Welcome to "Talk Like a Pro: Essential English Workplace Vocabulary for Success." This book is the culmination of a decade-long journey, filled with countless conversations and interactions with professionals and leaders from diverse multinational organizations. It is with great pleasure that I present this comprehensive collection of phrases, carefully curated to empower you with the tools to become a master communicator in the workplace.

In today's dynamic and interconnected business landscape, effective communication is the cornerstone of success. Whether you are navigating complex projects, collaborating with colleagues, or engaging with clients, the ability to articulate your thoughts, convey your ideas persuasively, and build meaningful connections is paramount. This book is designed to be your go-to reference, providing you with an extensive repertoire of phrases tailored to various workplace scenarios.

The chapters within this book are thoughtfully organized to address specific communication challenges and opportunities. Each chapter presents a wide range of phrases that you can readily utilize based on the situation at hand. From team meetings and negotiations to presentations and conflict resolution, you will find practical phrases to help you navigate through every professional interaction with confidence and finesse.

What sets this book apart is its foundation in real-world experiences. The phrases contained within these pages have been gathered from professionals and leaders across multinational organisations. They are tried-and-tested expressions that have proven their effectiveness in diverse workplace settings. Whether you are a seasoned professional or just starting your career, this book will serve as an invaluable resource to sharpen your communication skills and elevate your professional presence.

I must acknowledge the tremendous effort that went into compiling this vast collection. The countless conversations, the observation of communication nuances, and the dedication to capturing the most impactful phrases have all contributed to the creation of this comprehensive guide. It is my sincere hope that this book will provide you with the tools and confidence to become a true pro at workplace communication.

Remember, mastering effective communication is an ongoing journey. As you explore the chapters and immerse yourself in the phrases, I encourage you to adapt them to your unique style and context. Embrace the power of words, the art of connection, and the potential for transformation that lies within effective workplace communication.

I would like to express my deepest gratitude to Mark Dougan, Matthew Colley, Vidyut Shetty, and Usha Murali, whose inspiration and invaluable conversations played a pivotal role in shaping this book. Their remarkable expertise at communicating effectively has been instrumental in indirectly contributing to the content and vision of this work.

I would also like to extend my heartfelt appreciation to Shubhangi and Siddhesh for their invaluable assistance in finetuning and formatting the book. Their attention to detail, unwavering commitment, and creative input have elevated this project to new heights.

With this book in your hands, you are equipped with a comprehensive toolkit of phrases that will empower you to navigate the intricacies of workplace communication with finesse and confidence. I invite you to embark on this transformative journey and witness the positive impact that effective communication can have on your professional growth and success.

Best wishes

Ravikiran Reddy

CONTENTS

CHAPTER 6

Problem Resolution 50

CHAPTER 7

Project Management.................. 181

CHAPTER 9

CHAPTER 1

Assessment and Decision Making

PHRASES-

"Go With a Hard View" -

> **Meaning:** - To make a definitive and firm decision

> **Examples:** -

- ❖ "The CEO decided to go with a hard view and proceed with the merger."

- ❖ "After much deliberation, the board went with a hard view and decided to invest in the new technology."

"Sense Check" -

> **Meaning:** - To review or evaluate something to ensure it is reasonable or accurate

- ❖ "Before presenting the proposal to the board, we need to do a sense check to ensure it aligns with our company's mission and values."

- ❖ "We conducted a sense check of the data and found some errors in our analysis."

"Lay Of the Land"-

> **Meaning:** - Understanding the current situation

> **Examples:** -

- ❖ "Before making a decision, let's get the lay of the land first"

- ❖ "The new employee spent the first week observing and learning about the office dynamics to get the lay of the land."

"To Fall Through the Cracks"-

> **Meaning:** - Ensuring that no task, responsibility, or information is overlooked or neglected.

> **Examples:** -

- ❖ "Complete every item, and make sure nothing falls through the cracks."

- ❖ "In our team, we have a meticulous project manager who ensures that nothing falls through the cracks by closely monitoring deadlines and assigning clear responsibilities."

"My Point Still Stands"-

> **Meaning:** - The statement I made remains valid and unchanged.

> **Examples:** -

❖ "Despite the opposition's objections, my point still stands that our marketing strategy will increase sales."

❖ "Even after the team's feedback, my point still stands that we need to prioritise customer satisfaction over cost-cutting measures."

"To Be Torn"-

> **Meaning:** - If you are torn between two or more things, you cannot decide which to choose, and so you feel anxious or troubled.

> **Examples:** -

❖ "I am torn, I cannot decide whether to allocate the budget towards marketing or research and development for our new product launch."

❖ "I am torn, I cannot decide whether to promote employee A or employee B to fill the vacant managerial position."

"To Take Something with A Grain of Salt"-

> **Meaning:** - To understand that something is not completely true or right not take something too seriously

> **Examples: -**

* ❖ "I have read the article, but I take it with a grain of salt. "

* ❖ "When considering a new investment opportunity, I will take the financial projections with a grain of salt until I conduct thorough research."

"Goes Without Saying"-

> **Meaning:** - Something that is obvious or understood without needing to be stated explicitly.

> **Examples: -**

* ❖ "It goes without saying that lay appointees must be selected with care"

* ❖ "In project management, it goes without saying that clear roles and responsibilities contribute to successful outcomes."

"Old Duck in The Pond"-

> **Meaning:** - conveys the idea that someone's hard work and effort may go unnoticed or undervalued, similar to how an old duck appears calm on the water's surface while paddling vigorously underneath. It serves as a reminder not to judge others solely based on appearances and to recognize the hidden effort behind their achievements.

➤ **Examples: -**

❖ "Despite working tirelessly behind the scenes to ensure smooth operations, the IT support team is often seen as an "old duck in the pond" as their efforts to maintain the company's systems go unnoticed until a technical issue arises"

❖ "The marketing coordinator's extensive research and preparation for client presentations may seem effortless to others, akin to an old duck in the pond, as they flawlessly deliver impactful pitches without revealing the diligent effort put into crafting them."

"To Rest One's Case"-

➤ **Meaning:** - Conveying that all necessary evidence or arguments have been presented and there is no need for further discussion or debate.

➤ **Examples: -**

❖ "After presenting the data, analysis, and testimonials supporting my proposal, I rest my case regarding the implementation of the new marketing strategy."

❖ "Considering the extensive research and customer feedback, I rest my case on the need for additional resources to improve product quality."

"Spare Me Your Idealism"-

> **Meaning:** - Disregard your idealistic notions and focus on practical considerations.

> **Examples:** -

- ❖ "During a project meeting, when a team member suggests an ambitious but impractical idea, the project manager says, spare me your idealism; we need to consider the constraints and limitations we're facing."

- ❖ "In a boardroom discussion about budget allocation, a board member dismisses an overly optimistic proposal by saying, " Spare me your idealism; we need to make decisions based on concrete data and financial feasibility."

"To Play Ten-Dimensional Chess Here"-

> **Meaning:** - Employing complex and strategic thinking to navigate challenging situations.

> **Examples:** -

- ❖ "I am playing ten-dimensional chess here to assess all possible outcomes before making a crucial decision regarding our company's expansion."

- ❖ "In this high-stakes negotiation, I am playing ten-dimensional chess here, carefully considering every move to secure the best deal for our organization."

"The Next Feature Fallacy Toys with The Optimist in Us"-

- ➤ **Meaning:** - The tendency to priorities future features over current problems affects our optimistic outlook.

- ➤ **Examples:** -

  - ❖ "In project management, the next feature fallacy toys with our optimism, shifting focus away from critical issues to the excitement of upcoming enhancements."

  - ❖ "When discussing product development, the next feature fallacy plays with our optimistic mindset, causing us to overlook present shortcomings while fixating on enticing future possibilities."

"We Don't Need to Resurrect Old Adam to Tell Us That"-

- ➤ **Meaning:** - We don't need to revisit past decisions or individuals to understand the current situation or make informed choices.

- ➤ **Examples:** -

  - ❖ "During a project discussion, a team member suggests reconsidering an old approach. The project lead responds, we don't need to resurrect old Adam to tell us that. Let's focus on moving forward with our current strategy."

❖ "In a management meeting, someone brings up a previously failed initiative as a reference point. The CEO interrupts, saying, we don't need to resurrect old Adam to tell us that. Let's learn from our past but focus on finding new solutions for the present challenges."

CHAPTER 2

Communication And Collaboration

"Show of hands"

> **Meaning:** - Seek a quick vote or opinion

> **Examples:** -

- ❖ "Let's do a quick show of hands to see how many people support this proposal."

- ❖ "In a team meeting, the manager said, Let's do a quick show of hands to see who agrees with the proposed deadline extension."

"Conscious agreed interlocked decisions"

> **Meaning:** - Making decisions that are mutually agreed upon and coordinated

> **Examples:** -

- ❖ "We need to ensure conscious agreed interlocked decisions across departments to avoid any miscommunication."

- ❖ "In the boardroom, conscious agreed interlocked decisions were made regarding the company's budget allocation for the upcoming fiscal year."

"I second that"

> **Meaning:** - To express agreement or support for a proposal or

> **Examples:** -

- ❖ "During the team meeting, when John proposed implementing a new project management tool, Sarah said, I second that idea."

- ❖ "In the boardroom, when the CEO presented a motion to implement cost-cutting measures, I seconded that decision as it was crucial for the company's financial stability."

"We can spin into it"

> **Meaning:** - To turn a negative situation into a positive one through creative thinking and solutions

> ➤ **Examples:** -

> ❖ "The marketing team was able to spin the negative reviews into a positive PR campaign."

> ❖ "In the face of a sudden change in project requirements, we can spin into it by brainstorming innovative approaches and adapting our strategy accordingly."

"Looky-loo"

> ➤ **Meaning:** - Someone who is overly curious or nosy about a particular event or situation.

> ➤ **Examples:** -

> ❖ "During the team meeting, John was being a looky-loo, constantly peeking into his colleagues' notebooks to see what they were writing."

> ❖ "The CEO noticed a group of employees being looky-loos near the conference room, trying to catch a glimpse of the confidential documents being discussed inside."

"Cut to the chase"

> ➤ **Meaning:** - Get to the main point or crucial information quickly.

> ➤ **Examples:** -

> ❖ "During a meeting, instead of discussing irrelevant details, John said, Cut to the chase

and tell us the key findings of the market research."

❖ "The CEO asked the team to cut to the chase in their presentation and focus on the financial implications of the proposed project."

"To not sound curt"

➤ **Meaning:** - Not intending to be rude or short

➤ **Examples:** -

❖ "I didn't mean to sound curt, I was just in a rush"

❖ "In an email to my manager, I didn't mean to sound curt while providing feedback on a project, but it may have come across that way."

"To tone down the rhetoric"

➤ **Meaning:** - A phrase used to advise someone to use a more measured and moderate tone in their communication

➤ **Examples:** -

❖ "Your message is getting lost in the inflammatory language. You need to tone down the rhetoric."

❖ "During a team meeting, one team member is speaking loudly and aggressively. The manager says, You need to tone down the rhetoric."

"Give a download"

> **Meaning:** - To provide an update or share information with someone

> **Examples:** -

❖ "I'll give you a download on the project status after the meeting."

❖ "Before the presentation, I'll give you a quick download on the key findings from the market research"

"To throw a carrot"

> **Meaning:** - A phrase used to describe a way of persuading someone with an incentive or reward

> **Examples:** -

❖ "The salesperson said to the potential client, What incentives can I throw at you like a carrot to close this deal?"

❖ "During team meetings, managers want to throw at them like the carrot by highlighting the rewards and bonuses for achieving targets"

"Let me set the stage"

> **Meaning:** - Establishing the necessary background and conditions for a given situation.

➢ **Examples:** -

- ❖ "Let me set the stage for this meeting by providing an overview of the project's objectives and key milestones."

- ❖ "Before we discuss the proposal, let me set the stage by highlighting the market trends and competitive landscape."

"Great minds think alike"

➢ **Meaning:** - A phrase used to express that people who share similar ideas or ways of thinking will naturally work well together

➢ **Examples:** -

- ❖ "We were able to collaborate so easily because people with great minds think alike."

- ❖ "During a project review, team members with great minds think alike and provide insightful feedback and suggestions, fostering continuous improvement and excellence."

"Synergetic Relationship"

➢ **Meaning:** - Working together as team, getting each other's back, operating in harmony, these are all descriptions of what constitutes synergistic relationships

➢ **Examples:** -

- ❖ "The marketing and sales departments have a synergetic relationship, combining their efforts to create effective campaigns and drive revenue."

❖ "The project manager and the team members maintain a synergetic relationship, coordinating tasks and sharing ideas to ensure project success."

"They got the chocolate and we got peanut butter"

➢ **Meaning:** - Unequal distribution of resources or benefits.

➢ **Examples:** -

❖ "In the team project, they received all the necessary budget and equipment, while we were left with minimal resources. They got the chocolate and we got peanut butter."

❖ "During the merger negotiation, the other company obtained valuable intellectual property rights, while our side only received minor concessions. They got the chocolate and we got peanut butter."

"To Meet Half Way"

➢ **Meaning:** - A request for equal effort and compromise from both parties involved in a task or project.

➢ **Examples:** -

❖ "During a project, one team member asks another to contribute more effort by saying, can you meet me halfway, I have done so much?"

❖ "In a negotiation, one party requests a fair compromise from the other by stating, can you meet me halfway, I have done so much?"

"Don't Create Further Drift"

➢ **Meaning:** - To avoid misunderstandings or miscommunication

➢ **Examples:** -

❖ "The manager emphasised the importance of clear communication to the team and told them not to let anyone create further drift."

❖ "The project lead reminded the team to clarify any uncertainties and not let misunderstandings create further drift."

"Come Back On One's Thoughts"

➢ **Meaning:** - To indicate that further thoughts or feedback will be provided at a later time

➢ **Examples:** -

❖ "The team lead said, I need to think about this more. I will come back to you on my thoughts."

❖ "The manager replied, Thank you for your input. Let me review it and I will come back to you on my thoughts."

"Talking Point"

> **Meaning:** - Use something as a point of discussion or conversation

> **Examples:** -

- ❖ "Let's just use the new product launch as a talking point to get the conversation started."

- ❖ " During team meetings, if the conversation starts to stray off-topic, just use it as a talking point to steer the discussion back on track"

"Duck someone"

> **Meaning:** - To assure someone that one is not avoiding or ignoring them

> **Examples:** -

- ❖ "I'm not ducking you; I've just been busy with other projects."

- ❖ "I am not ducking you, but I need some time to gather all the necessary information before discussing the project."

"Hold Fire On That"

> **Meaning:** - To postpone or delay action on a decision or plan

> **Examples:** -

- ❖ "Let's hold fire on that until we have more information."

❖ "The project manager advised the team to hold fire on that proposal until we analyse the potential risks."

"Circle Back"

➢ **Meaning:** - To revisit a topic or issue

➢ **Examples**: -

❖ "Let's circle back to the budget discussion at the end of the meeting."

❖ "Let's circle back on the marketing campaign next week to discuss the updated metrics."

"Close The Loop"

➢ **Meaning:** - To complete a process or task by making sure that all parties involved have been informed and are aware of the status or outcome

➢ **Examples:** -

❖ "Let's close the loop on this project by scheduling a final meeting with the stakeholders to review the results."

❖ "Let's close the loop on the customer's feedback by addressing their concerns and offering a satisfactory resolution."

"To Build A Picture"

➢ **Meaning:** - Providing additional information or context to help understand a situation better

> **Examples:** -

  * ❖ "Just to build that picture, let me give you some background on the project."

  * ❖ "Let's gather market data and competitor insights, just to build that picture."

"To Put Sense Into Something"

> **Meaning:** - To provide clarity or understanding

> **Examples**: -

  * ❖ "Let me put some sense into you. We need to work on this together."

  * ❖ "During the team meeting, a colleague was confused about the project's objectives, so I said, Let me put some sense into you and explained the goals clearly."

"To Cut Down The Chase"

> **Meaning:** - To get straight to the point

> **Examples:** -

  * ❖ "Let's cut down the chase and get to the main topic."

  * ❖ "Let me cut down to the chase - we need to reduce production costs by 20% in the next quarter."

"To Have A Bead On Someone"

> **Meaning:** - To have a clear understanding or knowledge of someone's whereabouts or actions.

> **Examples:** -

   ❖ "I've got a bead on him. He's currently in the conference room, wrapping up a meeting. I'll let him know you're looking for him."

   ❖ "We're preparing for the client presentation tomorrow. Have you got a bead on him?"

"Let's Dive In"

> **Meaning:** - To start working on a task or project enthusiastically and without hesitation

> **Examples:** -

   ❖ "During a project kick-off meeting, the project manager declares, Now that we have the necessary resources, let's dive in and collaborate to achieve our goals."

   ❖ "We've discussed the project plan thoroughly, now let's dive in and execute it without delay."

"Kicking Off The Meeting"

> **Meaning:** - To start or begin a meeting

> **Examples:** -

   ❖ "The CEO took charge and kicked off the meeting with an inspiring speech."

   ❖ "The project manager kicked off the meeting by outlining the objectives and highlighting the key milestones to be achieved during the week."

"Marry Back"

- ➤ **Meaning:** - To align or connect two different ideas or concepts

- ➤ **Examples:** -

  - ❖ "We need to marry back the interest in AIIR to Wall Street reports to gain investor confidence."

  - ❖ "The company's situation demands to marry back the interest in AIIR to Wall Street reports for a unified understanding of market trends and financial forecasts."

"To Have A Narrative"

- ➤ **Meaning:** - To have a coherent and compelling story that ties together the company's mission, values, and goals

- ➤ **Examples**: -

  - ❖ "The marketing team developed a narrative that highlighted the company's commitment to sustainability and social responsibility."

  - ❖ "When presenting a project update, having a narrative helps to engage stakeholders and deliver key messages effectively."

"Let's Drink To It (On That Note)"

- ➤ **Meaning:** - I'll drink to that! means that one agrees completely with something that someone has said.

➤ **Examples: -**

❖ "After closing a major deal, the team gathered and said, Let's drink to it! as they raised their glasses in celebration."

❖ "At the annual company gala, the CEO made an inspiring speech, concluding with the words, Let's drink to it! as everyone toasted to another successful year."

"Some Of Them We Can Stomach And Some Of Them We Cannot"

➤ **Meaning:** - Refers to different actions or behaviours that occur in various situations, some of which we find tolerable while others we find unacceptable.

➤ **Examples: -**

❖ "In team meetings, some members' interruptions we can stomach and some we cannot."

❖ "When it comes to punctuality, minor delays we can stomach, but consistent lateness we cannot."

"No Reason To Stray"

➤ **Meaning:** - I had no justification to deviate from the established course of action.

> **Examples:** -

❖ "When presented with multiple options, I had no reason to stray from the agreed-upon decision."

❖ "Despite external pressures, I had no reason to stray from the company's strategic plan."

"Your Frustration Is Duly Noted"

> **Meaning:** - Your frustration has been recognized and acknowledged.

> **Examples:** -

❖ "During a team meeting, a colleague expresses their dissatisfaction with the lack of progress on a project. The team lead responds, "Your frustration is duly noted, and we will address the issues to ensure better results.""

❖ "An employee sends an email complaining about a delayed response from a colleague. The colleague replies with a brief acknowledgment, saying, "Your frustration is duly noted.""

"It's Always Nice to Be Invited To The Dance Even If You Don't Have The Right Shoes"

> **Meaning:** - It's always positive to be included in an event or situation, even if you lack the necessary resources or skills.

➢ **Examples: -**

❖ "It's always nice to be invited to the meeting even if you don't have the right background knowledge."

❖ "It's always nice to be invited to the project even if you don't have the right tools or software."

"Well, The Night Is Young"

➢ **Meaning:** - Embracing the potential for positive outcomes in any circumstance, especially early on.

➢ **Examples: -**

❖ "In a corporate meeting, when faced with unexpected challenges, someone says, Well the night is young, let's brainstorm alternative solutions and adapt our approach."

❖ "During a project that has encountered setbacks, a team leader motivates the team by stating, Well the night is young, we can still turn things around and achieve success by adjusting our strategies."

"Sounds Good to Me"

➢ **Meaning:** - Expressing agreement or acceptance of an idea or proposal.

> **Examples: -**

  ❖ "We've decided to move forward with the new marketing campaign. Does everyone agree? Sounds good to me."

  ❖ "The proposal to allocate more resources to meet the deadline sounds good to me."

"Now We Are Talking"

> **Meaning:** - To express enthusiasm or agreement with a statement or idea

> **Examples: -**

  ❖ "When the CEO announced the company's new growth strategy, the team responded with 'Now we are talking!'"

  ❖ "The team brainstormed ideas, and when we hit upon a breakthrough solution, we all agreed, Now we are talking."

"To Resonat With Someone Or Something"

> **Meaning:** - Expressing agreement or similarity in opinion

> **Examples: -**

  ❖ "I really resonate with what you said about the importance of work-life balance."

  ❖ "During the team meeting, when a colleague shared their experience with a challenging client, I resonated with what they said as I had faced a similar situation before."

"Throw Me A Bone."

> **Meaning:** - Provide me with a small help or opportunity for progress.

> **Examples:** -

  ❖ "Throw me a bone by sharing some insights that could help me solve this issue."

  ❖ "I've been struggling with this task. Can you throw me a bone by giving me some additional resources or guidance?"

"Be One's Guest"

> **Meaning:** - Used to express encouragement or allowance for someone else to take action.

> **Examples:** -

  ❖ "Can I take the conversation in a different direction... other person can respond: Please, be my guest"

  ❖ "Do you mind if I order another glass of wine?" B: "Not at all—be my guest."

CHAPTER 3

Corporate Management

"Golden Handshake"-

> **Meaning** :- A generous severance package offered to a high-level executive who is being forced out of their position

> **Examples :-**

  ❖ "The CEO received a golden handshake when he was asked to step down from his position."

  ❖ "The company offered a golden handshake to downsized employees as a gesture of appreciation for their dedication."

"Modus Operandi"-

> ➤ **Meaning** :- A specific method or approach to achieve a goal or objective

> ➤ **Examples :-**

  - ❖ "Our modus operandi is to always prioritise customer satisfaction."

  - ❖ "Our modus operandi for decision-making involves gathering data, analysing it thoroughly, and consulting key stakeholders before reaching a conclusion."

"Heightened Support"-

> ➤ **Meaning:-** Refers to an increase in the level of support provided to a customer or client, often in response to an issue or problem they are experiencing.

> ➤ **Examples :-**

  - ❖ "We need to provide heightened support to our top clients to ensure their satisfaction and loyalty to our brand."

  - ❖ "The manager provided heightened support to the team by allocating additional resources and offering guidance, resulting in improved productivity and morale."

CHAPTER 4

Marketing and Product Development

"To Infuse All Flavours"-

> **Meaning:** - Blending and incorporating diverse elements or perspectives in a holistic manner.

> **Examples:** -

❖ "In our team meetings, we focus on infusing all the flavours by actively seeking input from different departments and considering a wide range of ideas and perspectives."

❖ "The success of our project relied on infusing all the flavours, as we brought together experts from various fields to collaborate and ensure a comprehensive and innovative outcome."

"Commercially Articulate"-

> **Meaning:** - To clearly and effectively convey the benefits of a product or service

> **Examples:** -

- ❖ "We need to commercially articulate the benefits of our new product to the target audience."

- ❖ "The marketing team commercially articulates product benefits in their ad campaign."

"To Convince One of Our Run Pedigrees"-

> **Meaning:** - Prove one's worth or ability

> **Examples:** -

- ❖ "We need to convince CBA of our experience and qualifications in order to win the contract. We need to present our run pedigree to convince them."

- ❖ "In a presentation to the CBA, we must provide compelling evidence and data to convince them of our run pedigree in managing complex financial systems."

"To Feed The Frenzy"-

> **Meaning:** -To contribute or add to a state of excitement, chaos, or high energy in the workplace.

> **Examples:** -

❖ "The manager's decision to announce the surprise bonus only served to feed the frenzy among the employees, resulting in a lively and enthusiastic atmosphere."

❖ "The marketing team's release of a teaser video for the upcoming product launch only served to feed the frenzy among customers, generating even more anticipation and excitement"

CHAPTER 5

Personal and Development Skills

"To Cloud One's Judgement"-

> **Meaning:** - Making it difficult to make a clear decision

> **Examples:** -

❖ "The emotions of the situation were clouding my judgement, so I had to step back and assess the facts."

❖ "The pressure to meet tight deadlines is clouding my judgment, causing me to overlook potential risks."

"To Not Follow The Pack"-

> **Meaning :-** Refusing to conform to conventional choices or opinions.

> **Examples :-**

   ❖ "She's not content to simply follow the pack"

   ❖ "During the decision-making process, John considers alternative options instead of blindly following the majority, showing that at least he doesn't follow the pack."

"Hold On To One's Guns"-

> **Meaning:-** Stay firm and resolute in your convictions or choices.

> **Examples: -**

   ❖ "During the meeting, when faced with differing opinions, it's important to hold on to your guns and defend your proposed solution."

   ❖ "In negotiations, it's crucial to hold on to your guns and not compromise on your bottom line, ensuring the best outcome for your company."

"Chicken Out"-

> **Meaning:** -To back out or avoid making a difficult decision or taking necessary action.

> **Examples: -**

   ❖ "During a critical project meeting, the team leader had to make a tough call, but they chickened out and postponed the decision, causing delays and confusion."

❖ "The manager was supposed to address the team about the upcoming changes, but they chickened out at the last moment and delegated the task to someone else, undermining their leadership."

"Throw Hat In The Ring"-

➤ **Meaning :-** To decide to participate in something or apply for something

➤ **Examples :-**

❖ "John decided to throw his hat in the ring and apply for the managerial position."

❖ "Several candidates threw their hats in the ring for the vacant executive position, hoping to be selected for the role."

"Little Niggling Feeling"-

➤ **Meaning :-** worrying someone slightly or causing them slight pain, usually for a long time/bothersome or persistent especially in a petty or tiresome way

➤ **Examples :-**

❖ "He has a niggling hip injury, which has troubled him on and off over the past year."

❖ "During a board meeting, the CEO had a little niggling feeling about the proposed marketing strategy but chose to proceed anyway."

"Instincts Serve Better Than Rules"-

> **Meaning** :- Relying on personal intuition rather than established rules and conventions when making choices.

> **Examples :-**

❖ "In a high-pressure project, my instincts serve me better than rules and conventions, allowing me to make quick decisions that lead to successful outcomes."

❖ "When faced with ambiguous situations, my instincts serve me better than rules and conventions by guiding me towards innovative solutions that surpass traditional approaches."

"To Be Akin To A Horse With Blinders"-

> **Meaning** :- that only looks in one direction and ignores all else.

> **Examples :-**

❖ "In a project meeting, the team leader emphasises, My hope is that we are not akin to a horse with blinders and carefully weigh all the pros and cons before finalising our decision."

❖ "During a strategic planning session, a manager reminds the team, Let's ensure we have a broad perspective and avoid being akin to a horse with blinders, so we can make informed decisions that benefit the company as a whole."

"For One's Education"-

➢ **Meaning :-** The phrase is used to indicate that the particular situation or action is solely for the purpose of acquiring knowledge or gaining understanding.

➢ **Examples :-**

❖ "During the team meeting, I asked several questions to clarify the project requirements, emphasising that my curiosity is just for my education."

❖ "I volunteered to assist a colleague with their presentation, stating that my intention to observe and learn from the experience is just for my education."

"Get/Sink One's Teeth Into"-

➢ **Meaning :-** To become fully involved and invested in a project or task, often involving a high level of attention to detail.

➢ **Examples :-**

❖ "I'm really excited to sink my teeth into this new project, it's a great opportunity to use my skills and make a real impact on the company's success."

❖ "He is known for his ability to sink his teeth into complex problems and come up with innovative solutions."

"There Are No Elevators To Success, There Are Only Stairs"-

➢ **Meaning** :- Success is achieved through hard work and effort

➢ **Examples:-**

❖ "We need to put in the hard work and take the stairs to achieve our goals."

❖ "Achieving work-life balance is a journey of continuous improvement; it cannot be attained overnight. There are no elevators to success, there are only stairs."

"To Slur One's Words"-

➢ **Meaning** :- Speech is unclear or unintelligible.

➢ **Examples** :-

❖ "During the presentation, the CEO noticed, You are slurring your words, making it difficult for the audience to understand the message."

❖ "In a team meeting, the manager addressed a team member, You are slurring your words; please try to speak more clearly so everyone can follow along."

"To Live In One's Little World"-

> **Meaning :-**   used to say that someone seems to spend a lot of time thinking or imagining things, and does not seem to notice what is happening around them

> **Examples :-**

  ❖ "I tried to talk to him, but he was in his own (little) world and didn't seem to hear what I was saying."

  ❖ "Despite being part of the same team, John and Sarah often have difficulty understanding each other's ideas and opinions because they live in their own little world."

"None Of My Jokes Are Landing Today"-

> **Meaning** :-The failure of conveying intended humour or messages effectively.

> **Examples :-**

  ❖ "During the presentation, none of my jokes are landing today, making it difficult to engage the audience and convey key points."

  ❖ "In the team meeting, none of my jokes are landing today, creating an awkward atmosphere and hindering effective communication."

"To Outlast Someone"-

> **Meaning** :- The phrase implies a sense of perseverance and lasting power, indicating the one's belief in surpassing others over time.

> **Examples** :-

❖ "In a corporate takeover bid, despite initial doubts, the CEO successfully acquires the rival company and says, I told you I would outlast them."

❖ "In a demanding corporate environment, I persevered through difficult times and proved my longevity by consistently delivering results. I told you I would outlast them."

"To Be Very Taken With One's Efforts"-

> **Meaning** :- To be impressed or pleased with someone's work or achievements

> **Examples** :-

❖ "The client's wife expressed that she was very taken with our team's recent efforts"

❖ "During the team meeting, John said, "My wife has been very taken with your recent efforts, and she wanted me to convey her appreciation for your hard work on the project."

"Sorry, I Am A Little Zoned Out"-

> ➤ **Meaning** :- Apologising for being momentarily inattentive or distracted.

> ➤ **Examples :-**

>> ❖ "During a team meeting, someone says, "Sorry, I am a little zoned out. Could you repeat the last point?""

>> ❖ "While reviewing a document, a colleague apologises, "Sorry, I am a little zoned out. Can you go over that paragraph again?""

"To Never Spill One's Guts"-

> ➤ **Meaning:-** To never reveal sensitive or confidential information.

> ➤ **Examples :-**

>> ❖ "During the negotiation, I would never spill my guts about our maximum budget limit."

>> ❖ "As an employee, I would never spill my guts about the company's future plans to competitors."

"Fluid Intelligence"-

> ➤ **Meaning** :- Referring to one's ability to reason and solve problems in new situations

> ➤ **Examples :-**

>> ❖ "We need to hire someone with high fluid intelligence to handle this project."

❖ "During a brainstorming session, employees with high fluid intelligence can generate innovative solutions to complex challenges."

"Gold Fish Memory"-

➢ **Meaning** :- Short memory retention

➢ **Examples** :-

❖ "Sorry, I have a goldfish memory, could you remind me what we talked about yesterday?"

❖ "The manager's goldfish memory often leads to misunderstandings as he forgets previous discussions and agreements made during team meetings."

"To Be Spaced Out"-

➢ **Meaning** :- Feeling ignored or overlooked

➢ **Examples** :-

❖ "I feel like I'm being spaced out in team meetings."

❖ " In group brainstorming sessions, sometimes I'm spaced out, and my ideas go unheard or overlooked."

"To Hone In. "-

➢ **Meaning** :- To focus or concentrate on a specific aspect or task.

> **Examples :-**

  * "In a meeting, it's very important to hone in on the key objectives to ensure efficient decision-making."

  * "When reviewing documents, it's very important to hone in on the details to avoid any errors or oversights."

"To Be A Bit More Thorough"-

> **Meaning:** -Giving extra attention or care to ensure completeness and accuracy

> **Examples:** -

  * "We need to be a bit more thorough in our analysis before we present the report."

  * "We are being a bit more thorough in our product inspections to ensure high-quality standards are met before shipment."

"Stepping Over to A New Land"-

> **Meaning:** - To expand or venture into a new market or industry

> **Examples:** -

  * "The company is stepping over to Intellitracs land with their new product line."

  * "Stepping over to Intellitracs land, our organisation is venturing into untapped markets to broaden our product offerings and reach a wider customer base."

"Get A Run On The Board"-

> ➤ **Meaning** :- To achieve a significant or successful milestone for the first time

> ➤ **Examples** :-

>> ❖ "After the successful product launch, we finally got a run on the board and are ahead of our competitors."

>> ❖ "In preparation for the product launch, we need to get this testing underway to ensure its functionality and reliability."

"Stand Without Crutches"-

> ➤ **Meaning:** - To operate successfully without relying on a particular person, product, or strategy

> ➤ **Examples:** -

>> ❖ "Our business needs to be able to stand without crutches and survive any changes in the market."

>> ❖ "A true leader knows how to stand without crutches, make tough choices, and owning the outcomes without blaming others."

"To Stand At The Crossroads"-

> ➤ **Meaning:** - Being at a point of decision-making about the path to pursue after graduation.

➤ **Examples: -**

❖ "I was standing at the crossroads after my graduation, contemplating whether to join a corporate job or start my own business."

❖ "I was standing at the crossroads after my graduation, unsure whether to pursue further education or directly enter the workforce."

"Pick Your Rosebuds While You May"-

➤ **Meaning :-** Make the most of your opportunities while you have them.

➤ **Examples :-**

❖ "In a corporate setting, "Pick your rosebuds while you may" serve as a reminder to employees to seize opportunities for career growth and development, such as attending relevant training programs or taking on challenging projects."

❖ "When considering potential investments, "Pick your rosebuds while you may" implies the importance of taking advantage of favorable market conditions or lucrative opportunities before they disappear or become less advantageous."

"To Fall On One's Sword"-

➤ **Meaning :-** To fall on one's sword means to take responsibility for something that has gone wrong, in particular, to resign from one's position as a way to acknowledge responsibility for something that has gone wrong

➤ Examples :-

❖ "In a team project, when a mistake occurs, I am willing to acknowledge my part in it, but I am not falling onto my sword by accepting blame for the entire failure."

❖ "During a performance review, I am open to constructive criticism, but I am not falling onto my sword by accepting unjustified accusations or shouldering the blame for others' mistakes."

"Long Narrative"-

➤ **Meaning:** - Recognizing that one's explanation or story is lengthy

➤ **Examples**: -

❖ "Sorry, that's a long narrative, but I wanted to provide you with all the necessary details."

❖ "In the interest of time, I'll skip the long narrative and get straight to the main idea."

"To Age Like Fine Bananas"-

➤ **Meaning:-** Bananas spoil very quickly. "Aging like a fine banana" means that someone/something is not aging well at all.

> Examples:-

* ❖ "Despite the rapidly evolving market trends, the consultants' adaptability aged like fine bananas, leaving them ill-prepared for the shifting landscape."

* ❖ "The company's lack of investment in upskilling its workforce resulted in their adaptability aging like fine bananas, hindering their ability to embrace new technologies."

"I Love Someone Or Something To Pieces"-

> Meaning: - to truly adore someone or something

> Examples: -

* ❖ "After a successful project launch, I gathered my team and said, They are great, I love them to pieces!"

* ❖ "In a team meeting, I expressed my admiration by stating, They are great, I love them to pieces for their innovative ideas and hard work."

"Weird Hinge"-

> Meaning :- A perplexing or puzzling occurrence that deviates from the expected norm.

> Examples :-

* ❖ "In a corporate meeting, a strange and unexplained technical glitch disrupts the presentation, leaving everyone puzzled and

unsure how to proceed. This is a weird hinge situation."

- ❖ "An employee receives a cryptic and mysterious email from an unknown sender, causing confusion and speculation within the company. The unusual message creates a weird hinge situation, leaving people uncertain about its meaning and intent."

"To Be Fixated on Power"-

- ➢ **Meaning:** - An individual's excessive preoccupation with acquiring and maintaining authority or control.

- ➢ **Examples: -**

  - ❖ "In the corporate world, he was fixated on power, constantly seeking promotions and authority over others."

  - ❖ "His obsession with power hindered collaboration and teamwork, as he focused solely on asserting dominance rather than fostering a cooperative work environment."

"I Am Sorry I Was Out Of Line"-

- ➢ **Meaning :-** Expressing regret for inappropriate behaviour or actions.

- ➢ **Examples :-**

  - ❖ "During a meeting, I made an offensive comment. Later, I approached my colleagues and said, "I am sorry I was out of line.""

❖ "I sent an email with incorrect information to a client. To rectify the situation, I wrote a follow-up email, stating, "I apologise for the mistake in my previous email. I am sorry I was out of line.""

"Excuse My Rudeness"-

➤ **Meaning :-** Acknowledging and apologising for impolite behaviour in a corporate setting.

➤ **Examples :-**

❖ "During a meeting, when interrupting someone, you say, Excuse my rudeness, but I have an important point to add."

❖ "When accidentally speaking out of turn to a superior, you apologise, saying, Excuse my rudeness, I didn't mean to interrupt you."

"Precognitive Powers"-

➤ **Meaning :-** Precognition also called prescience, future vision, or future sight, is a claimed psychic ability to see events in the future.

➤ **Examples :-**

❖ "During our project meeting, you accurately predicted the potential risks we would face. Your precognitive powers amaze me."

❖ "In a strategic planning session, a team member accurately foresees a market trend that others overlooked, prompting you to exclaim, Your precognitive powers amaze me."

"I Am Thinking of Wearing the Mask As A Novelty."-

> **Meaning** :- the quality of being new and unusual:

> **Examples :-**

❖ "During a team-building event, I am thinking if wearing the mask as a novelty to encourage creativity and foster a lighthearted atmosphere."

❖ "In a corporate meeting, a colleague suggests the idea of wearing masks as a novelty to break the ice and create a more relaxed atmosphere for brainstorming sessions."

"To Embark On A Journey"-

> **Meaning** :- To begin or start a new endeavour or project, often with a sense of excitement or adventure.

> **Examples :-**

❖ "The company's decision to embark on a journey of digital transformation required extensive planning and resource allocation."

❖ "The team members were filled with anticipation as they embarked on a new project, ready to explore uncharted territory and achieve their goals."

CHAPTER 6

Problem Resolution

PHRASES-

"Project Image Of The Man He Wasn't"-

> **Meaning:** -Portraying oneself as someone different from who they truly are.

> **Examples:** -

- ❖ "During a job interview, John projected an image of the man he wasn't by exaggerating his qualifications and experiences to impress the interviewer."

- ❖ "In a corporate setting, Sarah projected an image of the woman she wasn't by pretending to be highly organised and detail-oriented, although she struggled with managing deadlines and prioritising tasks."

"Snowball Effect"-

> **Meaning:** - A situation where a small event or problem starts to grow and quickly gets bigger and bigger, becoming harder to control

> **Examples** :-

- ❖ "The negative PR snowball effect from the CEO's scandal is now threatening the company's survival."

- ❖ "In a brainstorming session, one innovative idea can have a snowball effect, inspiring others to contribute their own creative solutions and leading to breakthrough innovation."

"Cosmetic Changes"-

> **Meaning** :- Changes made to the appearance or branding of a company, without making significant changes to its operations or structure.

> **Examples:-**

- ❖ "The company underwent a cosmetic rebranding, changing their logo and colour scheme, but their core business remained unchanged."

- ❖ "The team implemented cosmetic changes to the website's design, but user engagement and conversion rates showed no significant improvement."

"Israeli Shelling"-

> **Meaning: -** Dealing with urgent and unexpected challenges.

> **Examples: -**

  ❖ "During the corporate crisis, the team exhibited resilience and adaptability, handling the Israeli shelling effectively."

  ❖ "The company implemented a robust crisis response plan to address the impact of Israeli shelling, ensuring employee safety and minimising operational disruptions."

"To Scrub A Sheet"-

> **Meaning :-** Review and clean up the data or information.

> **Examples :-**

  ❖ "Let's scrub this sheet to remove any duplicate entries and ensure the data is accurate before presenting it to the client."

  ❖ "Before sharing the report with the team, let's scrub this sheet to eliminate any confidential information."

"Smoke Screen (Cover-Up)"-

> **Meaning: -** If something that you do or say is a smokescreen, it is intended to hide the truth about your activities or intentions

> ➤ Examples: -

  - ❖ "He was accused of putting up a smokescreen to hide poor standards in schools."

  - ❖ "The sudden announcement of a new project is just a smoke screen to divert attention from the company's financial troubles."

"To Doctor Up Something"-

> ➤ **Meaning** :- Manipulating or altering something dishonestly or misleadingly.

> ➤ **Examples** :-

  - ❖ "In a corporate presentation, a colleague is accused of doctoring up a photograph to exaggerate the success of a project."

  - ❖ "During a marketing campaign, an employee is reprimanded for doctoring up a photograph to make a product appear more appealing than it actually is."

"Hold The Card Off the Sleeve"-

> ➤ **Meaning:** - Keeping a secret advantage or solution hidden until it is needed.

> ➤ **Examples:** -

  - ❖ "During a brainstorming session, one team member held the card off the sleeve and shared a brilliant idea that completely solved the problem."

❖ "The manager held the card off the sleeve by strategically withholding a key piece of information until the negotiation reached a critical point, giving the company an advantage."

"Chop Out Noise and Lift Only the Summary"-

➤ **Meaning** :- Eliminate unnecessary details and focus on the main points

➤ **Examples** :-

❖ "Can you please chop out all the noise and just lift only the summary of the report?"

❖ "During a team meeting, chop out all the noise and just lift only the summary of the key decisions made."

"To Snake Someone"-

➤ **Meaning** :- To deceive or betray someone's trust or expectations

➤ **Examples** :-

❖ "You snaked me by taking credit for my work in the meeting."

❖ "You snaked me by spreading rumours about me to the higher-ups."

"Full-Frontal Attack"-

➤ **Meaning** :- An aggressive or direct approach to solving a problem.

➤ **Examples :-**

❖ "Our company decided to launch a full-frontal attack on the market by drastically reducing prices"

❖ "In response to a decline in market share, the company executed a full-frontal attack by conducting extensive market research, redesigning their product line, and launching a robust marketing campaign to regain market dominance."

"Flash In The Pan"-

➤ **Meaning :-** A short-lived or fleeting success, that is not sustained over time.

➤ **Examples :-**

❖ "The new product release was a flash in the pan, generating a lot of initial interest but failing to maintain sales over the long term."

❖ "The new software was a flash in the pan - it generated excitement but didn't solve our underlying productivity issues."

"To Underscore The Seriousness Of The Situation"-

➤ **Meaning :-** Emphasising the severity or gravity of a difficult circumstance or problem.

- ➤ **Examples** :-

  - ❖ "During the project review, I did underscore the seriousness of the situation regarding our tight deadline and resource constraints."

  - ❖ "In the team meeting, I did underscore the seriousness of the situation in terms of the declining customer satisfaction ratings and the urgent need for improvement."

"Miles Away from Firming Up"-

- ➤ **Meaning** :- The decision or plan is not yet finalised or clear.

- ➤ **Examples** :-

  - ❖ "The new product launch strategy is some miles away from firming up, and we need to make a decision soon."

  - ❖ "The project timeline is some miles away from firming up, and we need to discuss and reach a final agreement."

"To Cloud One's Situation"-

- ➤ **Meaning** :- To confuse or complicate the process of making a decision.

- ➤ **Examples** :-

  - ❖ "During the team meeting, I didn't want to cloud your situation by introducing conflicting ideas and opinions."

* ❖ "I refrained from sharing my personal preferences so as not to cloud your situation and allow you to make an unbiased decision."

"Educated Decision"-

> **Meaning :-** Making a thoughtful and informed choice based on available information and analysis.

> **Examples :-**

* ❖ "Conducting thorough market research helps us to make an educated decision on product pricing."

* ❖ "Gathering input from all team members helps us to make an educated decision on project direction."

"Strategic Lens"-

> **Meaning :-** In any event or scenario, having a strategic lens is essential to make informed and thoughtful decisions.

> **Examples :-**

* ❖ "When evaluating potential investments, requires a strategic lens to assess risks, returns, and long-term implications."

* ❖ "Dealing with a workplace conflict requires a strategic lens to identify underlying issues, consider various perspectives, and find a mutually beneficial resolution."

"Commercial Construct"-

> **Meaning** :-The process of making choices or reaching conclusions in a business context.

> **Examples :-**

  - ❖ "The team engaged in a commercial construct to determine the best course of action for launching the new product."

  - ❖ "The board of directors held a commercial construct to decide on the allocation of resources for the upcoming fiscal year."

"Rolling The Dice"-

> **Meaning** :- Taking a chance or accepting a risk in a given situation.

> **Examples :-**

  - ❖ "In a corporate merger, the CEO said, "I think it's worth rolling the dice and pursuing this acquisition to expand our market presence.""

  - ❖ "During a project meeting, a team leader suggested, "I think it's worth rolling the dice and implementing this new technology to improve our efficiency, despite the potential challenges.""

"Tendency To Outfox "-

> **Meaning** :- A tendency to overthink or complicate decisions, resulting in self-imposed obstacles or difficulties.

- Examples :-

  - ❖ "John's tendency to outfox himself often leads to delays in project execution as he spends too much time analysing every detail."

  - ❖ "Mary's inclination to outfox herself hampers her ability to make quick decisions, causing missed opportunities in the competitive market."

"Naildown An Agreement"-

- Meaning :- Finalise and secure an agreement or understanding.

- Examples :-

  - ❖ "The team had a lengthy discussion to nail down an agreement on the project timeline."

  - ❖ "The negotiators worked tirelessly to nail down an agreement regarding the terms of the merger."

"Strong-Arm"-

- Meaning :- Forcing or pressuring someone to comply with a particular decision or course of action.

- Examples :-

  - ❖ "The manager strong-armed the team into accepting his proposal by threatening their job security."

❖ "The executive strong-armed the board members into approving the merger, disregarding their concerns and objections."

"Pin Down"-

➤ **Meaning:-** To clearly define or identify something

➤ **Examples :-**

➤ "The team had to pin down the scope of the project before they could start working on it."

➤ "The company had to pin down the requirements for the new software before selecting a vendor."

"Let Someone Cool One's Heels."-

➤ **Meaning** :- Allow someone to wait patiently without intervening or pressuring .

➤ **Examples :-**

❖ "During negotiations, if a team member is taking longer to respond to an offer, just let her cool her heels and give her the space she needs to make a decision."

❖ "If a colleague is feeling overwhelmed and needs time to gather her thoughts before addressing a mistake, just let her cool her heels and avoid adding unnecessary pressure."

"Kicking Down The Can"-

> **Meaning :-**   Postponing a decision or action

> **Examples :-**

 ❖ "The board of directors is just kicking down the can on the issue of succession planning."

 ❖ "The manager's habit of kicking down the can on addressing performance issues has led to a decline in team morale and productivity."

"To Pass The Torch"-

> **Meaning :-** To let someone else do the work that you were doing or support the ideas that you supported.

> **Examples :-**

 ❖ "The torch has been passed to the new generation."

 ❖ "In a project, if a team member demonstrates greater expertise in a certain task, it's wise to pass the torch and let them handle it for better outcomes."

"Walking On Eggshells."-

> **Meaning :-** be extremely cautious about one's words or actions/to be very careful not to offend or upset someone

> **Examples :-**

  ❖ "I was always on eggshells when my family came to stay."

  ❖ "In a workplace conflict, the supervisor had to walk on eggshells when addressing the issue with the employees involved, ensuring a fair resolution without escalating tensions."

"To Be Excused"-

> **Meaning :-** A polite way of asking if one may leave some place.

> **Examples :-**

  ❖ "During a meeting, the team lead says, You may be excused if you wish, allowing participants to leave if they feel their presence is not necessary."

  ❖ "At the end of a training session, the instructor says, You may be excused if you wish, giving attendees the choice to leave or stay for additional questions or discussions."

"To Not Sit Well with Someone or Something"-

> **Meaning :-** Something that doesn't match or align with someone's expectations, preferences, or values.

- ➤ **Examples :-**

  - ❖ "It doesn't sit well with me when team members don't contribute equally during a project."

  - ❖ "It doesn't sit well with me when important decisions are made without proper consultation with all stakeholders."

"To Go On A Rampage"-

- ➤ **Meaning** :- violent or excited behaviour that is reckless, uncontrolled, or destructive. a state of violent anger or agitation

- ➤ **Examples :-**

  - ❖ "The smallest mistake sends him into a rampage."

  - ❖ "The angry employee went on a rampage, throwing files and breaking office equipment, causing widespread chaos and halting productivity."

"To Have A Paper Trial"-

- ➤ **Meaning** :- To prefer having written records or documentation of something

- ➤ **Examples :-**

  - ❖ "I like to have a paper trail of all my transactions for my records."

* ❖ "In our company, we like to have a paper trail for all important decisions and transactions, ensuring accountability and clarity."

"To Hold Pen On The Scope"-

- ➢ **Meaning :-**   take responsibility.

- ➢ **Examples** :-

    - ❖ "As the project lead, Jessie holds the pen on the scope, taking ownership of defining and executing the project's objectives."

    - ❖ "When it comes to project deliverables, Jessie holds the pen on the scope, taking responsibility for ensuring all tasks are completed on time."

"Eem To Be Staged"-

- ➢ **Meaning :-**   Expressing skepticism or suspicion about the authenticity or genuineness of a situation.

- ➢ **Examples** :-

    - ❖ "During a corporate meeting, a presenter showcases exceptional sales figures, but someone says, I'm sorry but this seems very staged indicating doubt about the accuracy of the numbers."

    - ❖ "In a team-building activity, participants are asked to share personal stories, and someone responds, I'm sorry but this seems very staged suggesting that the stories feel rehearsed and not genuine."

"Draw A Line In The Sand"-

➢ **Meaning :-**   Setting clear boundaries or making a final decision about something

➢ **Examples :-**

❖ "The CEO drew a line in the sand and refused to compromise on the pricing strategy"

❖ "The team drew a line in the sand and decided to reject any proposal that did not align with the company's values."

"Phrase Of Wring"-

➢ **Meaning :-**   to squeeze or twist especially so as to make it dry or to extract moisture or liquid wring a towel dry.

➢ **Examples :-**

❖ "After washing their hands, they used the phrase of wring to squeeze out the excess water from the towel before hanging it to dry."

❖ "The phrase of wring was employed to extract the remaining juice from the citrus fruits, ensuring maximum utilisation in the recipe."

"Cut to the core of it"-

- ➢ **Meaning** :- Get to the essential or most important point quickly

- ➢ **Examples** :-

  - ❖ "Let's cut to the core of it and discuss the key findings of the report."

  - ❖ "We need to cut to the core of it and identify the root cause of the production delays to implement effective solutions."

"To turn crimson"-

- ➢ **Meaning** :- if someone goes or turns crimson, their face becomes red because they are embarrassed or angry

- ➢ **Examples** :-

  - ❖ "During the presentation, I turned crimson when the CEO pointed out my mistake."

  - ❖ "The new employee turned crimson when asked a challenging question during the team meeting."

"To not cry about what happened in kindergarten"-

- ➢ **Meaning** :- To not dwell on past experiences or setbacks

- ➢ **Examples** :-

  - ❖ "He told his team that he doesn't cry about what happened in kindergarten, and that they should learn from their mistakes and move on"

❖ "When discussing previous failures, the manager reminded the team, "Let's adopt a 'don't cry about what happened in kindergarten' attitude and concentrate on finding solutions for our present challenges.""

"Get cross"-

➤ **Meaning :-** To become angry or frustrated

➤ **Examples :-**

❖ "The client was getting cross over the delay in delivery of the product."

❖ "The negotiation between the two companies got heated, and both parties were getting cross over the terms of the partnership agreement."

"To lash out at someone"-

➤ **Meaning :-** Expressing remorse for losing control and reacting negatively towards someone in a corporate setting.

➤ **Examples :-**

❖ "My coach lashed out at me today"

❖ "I apologise for my behaviour earlier; I am sorry I lashed out at you during our discussion about deadlines."

"Tender-hearted"-

> **Meaning** :- Displaying empathy and compassion towards others.

> **Examples** :-

❖ "In a corporate setting, being tenderhearted means offering emotional support to a colleague who is going through a difficult time."

❖ "A tenderhearted approach in the workplace involves showing understanding and kindness when providing feedback to the team members, focusing on their growth and well-being."

"All suit and no substance"-

> **Meaning** :- Focusing on appearances rather than meaningful action or content.

> **Examples** :-

❖ "An executive who prioritises flashy presentations over thorough analysis and thoughtful decision-making is all suit and no substance."

❖ "A manager who presents grandiose plans but fails to follow through with practical implementation is all suit and no substance."

"Wear colours"-

> **Meaning :-** A phrase used to express hope for a former employee to return to the company

> **Examples :-**

  ❖ "The manager wrote in an email to a former colleague, Hope you will be wearing Luxoft colours soon again."

  ❖ "An executive said Hope you'll be back in Luxoft colours soon to a retired employee, expressing gratitude and openness to their potential involvement in future projects. "

"To give the idea wings"-

> **Meaning :-** Encouraging the exploration and implementation of innovative ideas.

> **Examples :-**

  ❖ "My mother's encouragement really gave wings to my career as an artist."

  ❖ "During a project review, a colleague suggested, We should give the idea wings and see if it can lead to a breakthrough solution."

"Don't sweat it"-

> **Meaning:-**To not worry or stress about something.

➤ **Examples :-**

❖ "Don't sweat it, mistakes happen and we'll fix it"

❖ "During a company-wide reorganisation, employees were reminded not to sweat the uncertainties and to focus on their work."

"To be full of beans"-

➤ **Meaning :-** To be lively and enthusiastic.

➤ **Examples :-**

❖ "During the team meeting, she was full of beans, actively participating and contributing ideas."

❖ "Despite the challenging project deadline, she remained full of beans, motivating her colleagues with her positive energy."

"To give purpose a fair footing"-

➤ **Meaning :-** Ensuring equal opportunity and consideration for the intended goal or objective.

➤ **Examples :-**

❖ "During the decision-making process, it is essential to give my purpose fair footing by carefully evaluating all available options."

❖ "In order to make fair and unbiased decisions, it is important for the team to give my purpose fair footing by considering multiple perspectives."

"Heartfelt apology"-

> **Meaning** :-   Sincere expression of regret for a mistake or oversight.

> **Examples** :-

❖ "After discovering the error in the financial report, the accountant issued a heartfelt apology to the management team."

❖ "The project manager sent a heartfelt apology to the client for the delay in delivering the final product due to unforeseen circumstances."

"To not barter with people's health"-

> **Meaning** :-   A phrase used to convey a strong commitment to ethical principles, especially in relation to the well-being of others

> **Examples** :-

❖ "We can't compromise on the safety protocols just to save some money. I don't barter with people's health."

❖ "During project planning, I don't barter with people's health by pushing unrealistic deadlines that would compromise the physical or mental well-being of the team members."

"Flawed moral fumbling toward enlightenment"-

> **Meaning** :- Engaging in imperfect ethical reasoning while striving for greater understanding.

> **Examples :-**

❖ "During a corporate board meeting, the executives engaged in flawed moral fumbling towards enlightenment as they discussed the ethical implications of a potential business partnership."

❖ "The team members demonstrated flawed moral fumbling toward enlightenment as they navigated a complex decision-making the process regarding resource allocation for a critical project."

"If your claims hold water"-

> **Meaning** :- Assessing the validity or credibility of someone's claims or statements.

> **Examples :-**

❖ "During the performance review, if your claims hold water, you will receive the promotion you're seeking."

❖ "In the board meeting, if your claims hold water, we will consider your proposal for expanding into new markets."

"We will call this a wash"-

> **Meaning :-** To consider a situation or outcome as neutral or inconclusive, without any significant positive or negative impact.

> **Examples :-**

- ❖ "After analysing the data, we will call this a wash, as the results show no clear advantage for either approach."

- ❖ "The marketing campaign had mixed results, so we will call this a wash and reassess our strategy for the next quarter."

"Pass the sniff test"-

> **Meaning :-** Ensuring that a proposal or idea is acceptable to those who have the power to approve or reject it

> **Examples :-**

- ❖ "Before presenting the new marketing campaign, make sure"

- ❖ "The new marketing campaign underwent rigorous scrutiny to ensure it aligned with the company's values and ethics, passing the sniff test for both internal stakeholders and customers."

"Paint the picture"-

> **Meaning :-** Providing a detailed explanation or description

> **Examples :-**

❖ "Let me paint the picture for you so you can understand the situation better."

❖ "Before we proceed, let me paint the picture of the current market conditions and competition, so we can make an informed decision on our pricing strategy."

"A fish rots from the head"-

> **Meaning :-** Problems within an organisation often stem from the top management.

> **Examples :-**

❖ "In a company with poor leadership, employees lack motivation and direction, leading to low productivity. A fish rots from the head."

❖ "When executives engage in unethical practices, it sets a negative tone throughout the organisation, ultimately damaging its reputation. A fish rots from the head."

"Good pickup"-

> **Meaning :-** A positive feedback or recognition

> **Examples :-**

  - ❖ "Great job on that project; that was a really good pickup."

  - ❖ "John's innovative idea was a really good pickup for the team's project, enhancing their overall productivity."

"To smooth rough edges"-

> **Meaning :-** To provide constructive criticism to someone in order to help them improve

> **Examples :-**

  - ❖ "I need to smooth some of my rough edges before the performance review."

  - ❖ "John attended a workshop to smooth some of his rough edges in communication and presentation skills."

"Sugarcoat something"-

> **Meaning :-**   Present information or criticism in a more positive or palatable manner.

> **Examples :-**

  - ❖ "During performance reviews, when addressing areas for improvement, you need to sugarcoat it to maintain motivation and encourage growth."

❖ "When giving feedback on a colleague's presentation, you need to sugarcoat it to avoid discouraging them and maintain a positive working relationship."

"Point taken"-

➤ **Meaning** :- Acknowledging and understanding the feedback given.

➤ **Examples** :-

❖ "During a performance review, the manager provides constructive criticism to an employee about their communication skills. The employee responds with Point taken, indicating that they understand and acknowledge the feedback."

❖ "In a team meeting, a colleague points out a mistake in a project plan. The project lead acknowledges the observation by saying Point taken, expressing their understanding and acceptance of the error."

"Gold standard"-

➤ **Meaning** :- The highest standard or level of excellence that serves as a reference point.

➤ **Examples** :-

❖ "The company's customer service is the gold standard in the industry, setting a benchmark for others to aspire to."

* ❖ "Our team's meticulous attention to detail and exceptional quality control have established our product as the gold standard in the market."

"Astronomical cost"-

> ➤ **Meaning :-** If you describe an amount, especially the cost of something as astronomical, you are emphasising that it is very large indeed.

> ➤ **Examples :-**

* ❖ "The office spaces are selling for astronomical prices."

* ❖ "The company's extravagant office renovations resulted in an astronomical cost, pushing them into a financial crisis."

"To have one's wallets out"-

> ➤ **Meaning :-** People are ready to make a payment or engage in a financial transaction.

> ➤ **Examples :-**

* ❖ "During the sales conference, the clients were impressed with our product, and now they have their wallets out, ready to place orders."

* ❖ "The investors were convinced by the business proposal, and now they have their wallets out, ready to invest in the company."

"Fit as a flea"-

> **Meaning** :- in good physical condition : very healthy and strong

> **Examples** :-

- ❖ "I feel (as) fit as a flea this morning. "

- ❖ "John was praised by his supervisor for being fit as a flea in his performance evaluation, demonstrating outstanding productivity and efficiency in his work."

"Wiggle room"-

> **Meaning:-** Margin for adjustment or negotiation.

> **Examples** :-

- ❖ "We need to finish the project by Friday, but we should allow some wiggle room in case unexpected issues arise."

- ❖ "During the negotiation, it's essential to leave some wiggle room for concessions and compromises to reach a mutually beneficial agreement."

"One-track mind"-

> **Meaning** :- Being excessively focused on one particular aspect or goal.

> **Examples** :-

- ❖ "My sister has a one-track mind, only thinking about how something can further her career"

- ❖ "John, you have a one-track mind. You're so focused on perfecting that report, but you're ignoring the urgent emails waiting in your inbox."

"Dig a rabbit hole"-

- ➢ **Meaning :-** Need to focus on the most important issues/tasks

- ➢ **Examples :-**

  - ❖ "We can't keep digging every rabbit hole or searching every rabbit hole. Let's prioritise our efforts."

  - ❖ "To ensure efficient decision-making, we can't keep digging every rabbit hole during board discussions and must stay focused on strategic objectives."

"To funnel the money or something"-

- ➢ **Meaning :-** The act of directing or controlling the flow of money within a specific context or organization.

- ➢ **Examples :-**

  - ❖ "The accountant was investigated for possibly funneling company funds into his own accounts"

  - ❖ "During the audit, the team discovered irregularities in the accounts, leading to suspicions of embezzlement. You think he is funneling the money somehow."

"Embodiment of free speech"-

> **Meaning** :- The expression of ideas and opinions without fear of censorship or retaliation.

> **Examples** :-

❖ "In a boardroom meeting, each member freely expresses their thoughts and opinions, creating an embodiment of free speech that fosters better decision-making."

❖ "During a brainstorming session, employees are encouraged to voice their ideas and engage in open discussions, creating an embodiment of free speech that promotes innovation and creativity."

"To wipe the slate clean and start over"-

> **Meaning** :- To reset and begin anew without any past issues or mistakes.

> **Examples** :-

❖ "After a failed project, the team decided, Let's wipe the slate clean and start over to approach it with a fresh perspective and improved strategies."

❖ "In a meeting filled with tension and disagreements, the manager suggested, Let's wipe the slate clean and start over to foster a more positive and productive discussion."

"Right as rain"-

> **Meaning** :- Completely satisfactory or reliable.

> **Examples** :-

❖ "After thorough testing and evaluation, the new security system is working right as rain, providing complete assurance for the company's assets."

❖ " The team resolved their conflicts, and the project progressed smoothly, right as rain."

"To brave the seas"-

> **Meaning** :- Your efforts and perseverance will not go to waste.

> **Examples** :-

❖ "After months of hard work and late nights, you successfully completed the project. You did not brave the seas for nothing."

❖ "Despite facing numerous challenges and setbacks, your team managed to surpass the targets. You did not brave the seas for nothing."

"Opt for the herd"-

> **Meaning** :- The individual chose to conform to the majority opinion or follow the crowd without critical thinking.

> **Examples :-**

  ❖ "During the strategy meeting, when asked for his opinion, John remained silent and later agreed with the majority without providing any input. Looks like he opted for the herd."

  ❖ "Despite recognizing the flaws in the proposed project, Sarah went along with the team's unanimous decision rather than voicing her concerns. Looks like she opted for the herd."

"Every kitten grows up to be a cat"-

> **Meaning :-**   Every individual's potential can be realized with time and experience.

> **Examples :-**

  ❖ "The company invests in training programs to ensure that every kitten grows up to be a cat, fostering professional development and career advancement."

  ❖ "A team leader reminds the members that their current performance levels are not final and encourages them to embrace learning opportunities, stating Remember, every kitten grows up to be a cat."

"To wring one's hands"-

> **Meaning :-** clasp and twist one's hands together as a gesture of great distress, especially when one is powerless to change the situation.

> Examples :-

- ❖ "she was wringing her hands in agitation"

- ❖ "During the company's financial crisis, employees would often be seen wringing their hands, feeling powerless to prevent impending layoffs."

"Big ticket items"-

> Meaning :- Important or significant matters

> Examples :-

- ❖ "We need to focus on those big tickets and prioritise them first"

- ❖ "Those are big tickets, we need to carefully assess the potential ROI before committing"

"To exist since the stone age"-

> Meaning :- used to describe something that is very basic, simple, and not well developed/ OR VERY ANCIENT

> Examples :-

- ❖ "The lack of diversity in the company's leadership was a result of an outdated mindset—it was there since the stone age."

- ❖ "The importance of effective communication was there since the stone age, and it remains crucial for successful teamwork in the workplace."

"Put one's hand at heart"-

- ➤ **Meaning** :- To swear by one's honesty or sincerity

- ➤ **Examples** :-

  - ❖ "I assure you that the figures provided are accurate, if I have to put my hand at heart."

  - ❖ "If I have to put my hand at heart, I can assure you that the project will be delivered on time"

"Bury one's head in the sand"-

- ➤ **Meaning** :- to ignore a problem or an unpleasant situation and hope that it will disappear

- ➤ **Examples** :-

  - ❖ "Her parents had been burying their heads in the sand about the problem"

  - ❖ "In a corporate meeting, when confronted with a critical issue, the team leader decided to bury their head in the sand and dismiss any concerns raised."

"To live in lala land"-

- ➤ **Meaning** :-Refusing to acknowledge or deal with a difficult or unpleasant reality

- ➤ **Examples** :-

  - ❖ "It's time to stop living in lala land and start facing the harsh truth of the situation."

❖ "The manager's decision to invest in a failing company shows they are living in lala land."

"To leave an indelible mark"-

> **Meaning :-** Having a lasting impact or influence on others through one's actions or decisions in a corporate work environment.

> **Examples :-**

❖ "The CEO's innovative strategies and visionary leadership left an indelible mark on the company's growth and success."

❖ "His exceptional mentoring skills and ability to inspire his team members left an indelible mark on their professional development and motivation."

"Blown Away"-

> **Meaning :-** To be impressed or surprised by something

> **Examples :-**

❖ "I was blown away by the level of detail in their presentation."

❖ "The investors were blown away by the startup's growth projections."

"Constructive challenge"-

> **Meaning :-** To offer constructive criticism and suggestions for improvement

➢ **Examples** :-

❖ "We need to offer constructive challenge to the existing plan to ensure its success."

❖ "During a team meeting, a colleague offers constructive challenge to a project proposal, highlighting areas that need further development."

"Bumbling idiot"-

➢ **Meaning** :- Refers to a person who consistently demonstrates incompetence or lack of skill in various work-related situations.

➢ **Examples** :-

❖ "During the team meeting, John failed to provide any valuable input and struggled to understand the discussion points, making him appear like a bumbling idiot."

❖ "Sarah's constant mistakes and inability to follow simple instructions labeled her as the office bumbling idiot among her colleagues."

"To be someone's training wheels"-

➢ **Meaning** :- To assist others in their basic learning or development.

➢ **Examples** :-

❖ "In a team project, I won't have time to guide my colleagues step-by-step. I don't have time to be anyone else's training wheels."

❖ "As a manager, I need my employees to take ownership of their tasks and learn independently. I don't have time to be anyone else's training wheels."

"Half idiot"-

➢ **Meaning** :- A humorous way of expressing that someone is not very smart

➢ **Examples** :-

❖ "I forgot my keys again, I must be a half idiot, joked the employee."

❖ "Interrupting others during a meeting is a display of half-idiot meeting etiquette"

"Give someone time to assimilate this information"-

➢ **Meaning** :- Allow sufficient time for understanding and incorporating new information.

➢ **Examples** :-

❖ "Before making any decisions, I will give you time to assimilate this information."

❖ "Our team will provide a presentation to give stakeholders time to assimilate this information before proceeding with the project."

"To fill someone in"-

> **Meaning** :- Sharing confidential or sensitive information about an individual or organisation without their consent or proper authorization.

> **Examples** :-

❖ "A colleague threatened to fill in the WhiteHouse with my personal details as a way to intimidate and gain an advantage in a negotiation."

❖ " The disgruntled employee vowed to fill in the WhiteHouse with company secrets as an act of revenge against the management."

"To be classified"-

> **Meaning:** - Topic might be sensitive or confidential

> **Examples** :-

❖ "During a meeting, a colleague mentioned a project code name that I wasn't familiar with. I thought it might be classified, so I didn't ask for more details."

❖ "My manager hinted at upcoming organisational changes, but I sensed it might be classified information, so I didn't inquire further."

"To have less than a perfect answer"-

> **Meaning :-** means not very good.

> **Examples :-**

* ❖ "I have less than a perfect answer, but we're adapting to changing circumstances."

* ❖ "In a meeting, when asked about a technical issue, the engineer replied, I have less than a perfect answer, but I'm investigating the problem."

"To be officially intrigued"-

> **Meaning :-** A state of curiosity or interest aroused by the sharing of new information.

> **Examples :-**

* ❖ "During a team meeting, a colleague presents groundbreaking research finding, and you say, Now I am officially intrigued."

* ❖ "The CEO unveils a strategic plan for a major company expansion, and you lean forward, stating, Now I am officially intrigued."

"Name drop someone"-

> **Meaning :-** Mentioned your name to someone in a conversation.

> **Examples :-**

- ❖ "During the meeting, I also name dropped you, Mark, to emphasise your expertise on the subject."

- ❖ "I had a discussion with the team about the project, and I also name dropped you, Mark, to highlight your contribution."

"Transition on front foot"-

> **Meaning** :- Taking proactive measures to move forward

> **Examples :-**

- ❖ "The company needs to transition a bit more on the front foot to stay ahead of the competition."

- ❖ "To achieve our targets, we need to transition a bit more on the front foot by actively pursuing new market opportunities."

"It's very telling."-

> **Meaning** :- Indicates important information or reveals a significant aspect.

> **Examples :-**

- ❖ "During the presentation, the client's reaction was very telling."

- ❖ "The employee's consistent lateness to meetings is very telling about their lack of commitment."

"It was an all-nighter"-

> **Meaning :-** Engaging in an extended period of concentrated work or activity.

> **Examples :-**

* ❖ "It was an all-nighter as we prepared for the major presentation, working tirelessly to perfect our slides and rehearse our speeches."

* ❖ "It was an all-nighter to meet the project deadline, with the team collaborating nonstop to ensure the deliverables were completed on time."

"And the butchery begins"-

> **Meaning :-** A phrase used to describe the start of a difficult or unpleasant task or situation

> **Examples :-**

* ❖ "As soon as the audit began, the staff knew it was going to be a long day. And the butchery begins."

* ❖ "In a boardroom, executives clash over budget allocations, and the butchery begins as each side tries to defend their department's interests."

"Self-righteousness anger"-

> **Meaning :-** A situation where individuals assert their moral superiority with anger, causing tension and hostility.

> **Examples :-**

- ❖ "In a team meeting, a colleague expresses self-righteousness anger towards a coworker's suggestion, belittling their ideas and dismissing their input."

- ❖ "During a performance review, a manager displays self-righteousness anger by criticising an employee's work without considering their perspective or offering constructive feedback."

"To door-step someone or something"-

> **Meaning :-** When someone unexpectedly approaches or confronts you in an intrusive manner at work.

> **Examples :-**

- ❖ "She was doorstepped by a salesman"

- ❖ "During a team meeting, my manager door-stepped me to inquire about a project, diverting the attention of everyone present."

"No free lunches"-

> **Meaning :-** to mean you cannot expect to get things for nothing.

> **Examples :-**

- ❖ "When choosing a new business strategy, remember that there are no free lunches—

each option has its own set of advantages and drawbacks."

❖ "When selecting a marketing strategy, we must consider the potential risks and benefits because there are no free lunches in terms of guaranteed success or minimal effort."

"Get to the bottom of something"-

➤ **Meaning** :- to find out the true reason for or cause of (something)/to discover the real but sometimes hidden reason that something exists or happens

➤ **Examples :-**

❖ "During an audit, the financial team must get to the bottom of discrepancies in the accounting records to ensure accuracy and compliance."

❖ "When a project is behind schedule, the project manager must get to the bottom of the delays to identify the causes and take corrective actions."

"Lifting the hood"-

➤ **Meaning :-** Examining or investigating the inner workings or details of something

➤ **Examples :-**

❖ "The team spent the day lifting the hood on the engineering process to find areas for improvement."

❖ "Lifting the hood on engineering revealed a software bug that was causing system crashes."

"Quell the tensions"-

> **Meaning** :- Resolving conflicts or disputes effectively.

> **Examples** :-

❖ "The team leader quelled the tensions between two coworkers by facilitating a constructive dialogue and finding a compromise."

❖ "The HR manager quelled the tensions in the workplace by implementing a fair and transparent conflict resolution process."

"To be over one's head"-

> Meaning :- Not capable or qualified for the task

> Examples :-

❖ "She was promoted to the position without proper training and is struggling to keep up. It seems like she is definitely over her head."

❖ "She is definitely over her head managing the project's budget without any prior financial experience."

"By virtue of it"-

> **Meaning** :- By the strength or power of something, often

> **Examples :-**

  ❖ "By virtue of its professionalism, the company was able to establish long-term partnerships with reputable clients."

  ❖ "By virtue of their punctuality and dedication, the team members consistently delivered high-quality work."

"Lack of backbone"-

> **Meaning** :- A leader who lacks the necessary courage, determination, and resilience to make tough decisions and stand up for what is right.

> **Examples :-**

  ❖ "The team is losing faith in their manager as they perceive him to be spineless and incapable of making the necessary changes."

  ❖ "The team's lack of backbone in decision-making resulted in prolonged discussions and delayed project progress."

"To play catch-up "-

> **Meaning** :- To try to reach the same level of understanding, accomplishment, etc. as others, typically after a late start.

> **Examples :-**

  ❖ "Thanks to our terrible start, we've been playing catch-up all season."

❖ "I am playing catch up here with the new software system implementation."

"Intellectually curious"-

➤ **Meaning :-** Being open to acquiring knowledge and seeking understanding.

➤ **Examples :-**

❖ "In a corporate training session, employees who are intellectually curious actively engage in asking questions and exploring new concepts."

❖ "A team leader encourages intellectual curiosity among team members by promoting self-learning and providing opportunities for personal growth."

"Get into Muscle Memory"-

➤ **Meaning :-** Refers to a stage in the learning process when a skill or information becomes automatic or second nature

➤ **Examples :-**

❖ "Don't worry if you're struggling with the new software now, after a week or two of using it, everything will start getting into the muscle memory."

❖ "At first, it was hard to remember everyone's names, but after a few weeks on the job, it became second nature and everything started getting into the muscle memory."

"Cease and desist"-

> **Meaning :-** An order to stop doing something, typically from a legal authority

> **Examples :-**

❖ "We received a cease-and-desist order from the copyright owner."

❖ "The company's legal team issued a cease-and-desist order to prevent a competitor from using their trademarked logo"

"Cut some slack"-

> **Meaning :-** Allowing for mistakes or errors

> **Examples :-**

❖ "We should cut her some slack as she is new to the job"

❖ "During the performance review, let's cut some slack for John's recent mistakes as he has been dealing with personal issues."

"To go out of the window"-

> **Meaning :-** The loss of order, discipline, or structure in a given situation.

> **Examples :-**

❖ "During a crisis, if the team leader panics, everything will go out of the window, and chaos will ensue."

* ❖ "When a project lacks clear objectives and direction, everything will go out of the window, and productivity will suffer."

"Over engineer"-

➢ **Meaning :-** To avoid unnecessarily complicating a process or solution

➢ **Examples :-**

* ❖ "Let's keep this report simple and straightforward. I don't want to over engineer it."

* ❖ "During the report presentation, John emphasised, I don't want to over-engineer this report, let's focus on the key findings."

"Need to watch the jacket"-

➢ **Meaning :-** The management team's ability to adapt to change

➢ **Examples :-**

* ❖ "The company has implemented a new remote work policy, and we need to assess how the leadership team is adapting to the new style of work. Do they still feel the need to watch the jacket?"

* ❖ "How is the leadership team coping with the new style of work, do they still feel the need to watch the jacket during virtual meetings?"

"To herd cats"-

> ➤ **Meaning** :- A futile attempt to control or organise a class of entities which are inherently uncontrollable—as in the difficulty of attempting to command individual cats into a group (herd)

> ➤ **Examples :-**

>> ❖ "In a project with multiple stakeholders, coordinating their conflicting demands is like herding cats."

>> ❖ "Getting all the stakeholders aligned and moving in the same direction during a project is akin to herding cats."

"To play someone"-

> ➤ **Meaning** :- means someone is deceiving or exploiting you for their own benefit.

> ➤ **Examples :-**

>> ❖ "In the workplace, if your colleagues constantly provide misleading information to make you appear incompetent, they are playing you."

>> ❖ "When a manager assigns you a project with impossible deadlines and then blames you for not completing it on time, they are playing you."

"Won't cut ice in the market"-

> **Meaning :-** Not meeting the expectations or demands of the market.

> **Examples :-**

- ❖ "The outdated technology of our product will not cut ice in the market."

- ❖ "Without a competitive pricing strategy, our new service will not cut ice in the market."

"A rising tide lifts all boats"-

> **Meaning :-** When the economy or industry as a whole is doing well, all businesses within that sector tend to benefit

> **Examples :-**

- ❖ "Our company's revenue is up 15% this quarter, but so are our competitors'. It looks like a rising tide is lifting all boats."

- ❖ "Investing in employee growth benefits the entire company - a rising tide lifts all boats."

"Bring something to the forefront of mind"-

> **Meaning :-** Raising awareness of a product or brand in a customer's mind

Examples :-

- ❖ "Our new ad campaign aims to bring Teradata to the forefront of our customers' minds."

* "During the industry conference, the marketing team's goal was to bring Teradata to the forefront of attendees' minds by showcasing the company's innovative solutions."

"Bells and whistles"-

> **Meaning** :- Additional features or decorations that are not necessary but are added to make something more attractive or appealing.

> **Examples** :-

* "The new car model has all the bells and whistles like a sunroof, heated seats, and a touchscreen display."

* "Our company's latest software update includes all sorts of bells and whistles like customizable dashboards and new data visualisations."

"Normalise into rates"-

> **Meaning** :- Converting data or information into standardised rates for analysis or comparison.

> **Examples** :-

* "In financial analysis, we normalize into rates to assess the profitability of different investments on an equal basis."

* "When evaluating employee performance, we normalise into rates to fairly compare

productivity levels across different teams or departments."

"Blatant sensationalism"-

> **Meaning:-** Deliberate exaggeration and distortion in media reports to gain attention or provoke emotional reactions.

> **Examples :-**

❖ "The news article was filled with blatant sensationalism, exaggerating the impact of the company's financial loss to attract more readers."

❖ "The PR team criticised the journalist for resorting to blatant sensationalism in their reporting, distorting facts and damaging the company's reputation."

"Any other business?"-

> **Meaning :-** A common phrase used at the end of a meeting to ask if anyone has any additional items to discuss

> **Examples :-**

❖ "The chairperson of the meeting asked, Any other business guys, ok, we will wrap up then?"

❖ "The manager concluded the meeting by asking, Any other business guys, ok, we will wrap up then?"

"Interlock session"-

> **Meaning :-** A meeting where multiple teams come together to discuss a project or issue

> **Examples :-**

  ❖ "Let's schedule an interlock session to ensure all teams are on the same page."

  ❖ "During the interlock session, the marketing and sales teams discussed their strategies and identified opportunities for collaboration on upcoming campaigns."

"To be blanked"-

> **Meaning :-** To forget something completely

> **Examples :-**

  ❖ "I completely blanked on the client's name during the meeting"

  ❖ "When asked about the project details, I completely blanked and couldn't recall any specific information."

"Don't stick your nose"-

> **Meaning :-** Mind your own business and don't interfere with other's affairs

> **Examples :-**

  ❖ "I suggest you don't stick your nose where it doesn't belong and let the legal team handle this."

❖ "It's best not to stick your nose in office politics; stay neutral and focused on your work."

"To be not in a lyric writing workshop"-

➢ **Meaning:-** We should focus on clear and effective communication rather than using elaborate or ambiguous language.

➢ **Examples :-**

❖ "During a team meeting, someone starts using flowery language to describe a simple task. The team lead interjects, Not a lyric workshop. Let's keep it concise."

❖ "In a presentation about financial projections, an employee begins using poetic metaphors. The manager interrupts, saying, This isn't a lyric writing workshop. Stick to the facts."

"To blindside someone"-

➢ **Meaning** :- To catch someone off guard or surprise them with unexpected information or actions.

➢ **Examples :-**

❖ "I am sorry to blindside you, but the project deadline has been moved up by a week."

❖ "I am sorry to blindside you, but the client decided to cancel the deal at the last minute."

"To leave a lot of money on the table"-

> **Meaning :-** Failing to capitalise on a valuable chance or potential gain.

> **Examples :-**

❖ "During negotiations, by not pushing for better terms, you left a lot of money on the table."

❖ "By not investing in market research, we left a lot of money on the table when launching our product."

"To rub one's nose into something"-

> **Meaning :-** To force someone to confront and take responsibility for their mistakes or shortcomings.

> **Examples :-**

❖ "He beat us all in the race and then rubbed our noses in it."

❖ "During the team meeting, the manager rubbed my nose in it by highlighting my error in front of everyone."

"Sordid errors"-

> **Meaning :-** Unpleasant or shameful mistakes.

➤ **Examples :-**

❖ "In the meeting, the speaker made sordid errors in the financial presentation, causing confusion among the attendees."

❖ "The new employee's sordid errors in data entry led to significant delays and errors in the project deliverables."

"To bark up the wrong tree"-

➤ **Meaning :-** Accusing someone of pursuing the wrong course of action

➤ **Examples :-**

❖ "If you think he's the one responsible, you're barking up the wrong tree."

❖ "I think you are barking up the wrong tree. Our financial analyst would be the best person to answer your budget-related queries."

"I thought I made myself clear"-

➤ **Meaning :-** Expressing frustration when one's message or instructions were not understood as intended.

➤ **Examples :-**

❖ "During a project meeting, a team member fails to deliver the required report. The team leader says, I thought I made myself clear about the deadline for submitting the report."

❖ "In an email exchange, a manager asks an employee to complete a task by the end of the day, but the employee fails to do so. The manager responds, I thought I made myself clear about the urgency of completing the task."

"To hold someone for ransom"-

➢ **Meaning :-** Assuring someone that you are not intentionally causing harm or holding them back.

➢ **Examples :-**

❖ "We're being held to ransom by these extremist groups."

❖ "I understand we have different opinions, but I am not holding you for ransom because of it. Let's find a compromise."

"Fleeting glimpse"-

➢ **Meaning :-** something that happens really fast, or something that doesn't last as long as you'd like/If you get a glimpse of someone or something, you see them very briefly and not very well.

➢ **Examples :-**

❖ "During the presentation, the manager caught a fleeting glimpse of the competitor's new product design."

❖ "As I walked by, I had a fleeting glimpse of the CEO discussing the future plans with the board members."

"Martial music"-

➤ Meaning :-   Refers to music or sounds that evoke a sense of motivation, discipline, or urgency

➤ Examples :-

❖ "The coach played martial music during the halftime break to motivate the team for the second half."

❖ "During the company's annual kickoff meeting, martial music was played to inspire employees and set the tone for the new year."

"To have some music in one"-

➤ **Meaning :-**   Despite challenges or setbacks, the individual has untapped potential and a desire to contribute.

➤ **Examples :-**

❖ "In a team meeting, an employee expresses their dedication to the project, stating, There is still some music in me, and I'm committed to finding a solution."

❖ "In a team brainstorming session, the employee says, There is still some music in me. I have a few innovative ideas for this project."

"To get blood pumping"-

> **Meaning :-** Feeling energised and motivated.

> **Examples :-**

❖ "Got my blood pumping when I received recognition for my hard work during the team meeting."

❖ "Completing a challenging project on time got my blood pumping and boosted my confidence."

"To blow the interview"-

> **Meaning :-** Used to tell someone that you made a big mistake

> **Examples :-**

❖ "I think I might have messed up on a few questions so I think I blew it. "

❖ "You blew the interview? You didn't review your own resume and couldn't answer basic questions about your experience."

"Use the cards upon one's sleeve"-

> **Meaning :-**To use one's hidden resources or advantages to achieve a goal

> **Examples :-**

❖ "I have a few tricks up my sleeve that could help us close the deal."

❖ "When facing tough competition, use the cards that I have upon my sleeve to showcase unique strengths and outperform rivals in the market."

"Wriggle room"-

➢ **Meaning** :- Avoiding allowing any room for negotiation or changing the terms of a contract.

➢ **Examples** :-

❖ "We need to be firm with our suppliers and not give them any wriggle room in our contract negotiations."

❖ "During the contract negotiations, make sure to be firm and assertive, ensuring that you don't give them any wriggle room on the terms and conditions."

"Come to a middle ground"-

➢ **Meaning** :- Willingness to compromise for the sake of long-term gains

➢ **Examples** :-

❖ "Although we had different opinions on the budget, we were happy to come to a middle ground for any longer-term benefits for the company."

❖ "The two companies were able to find common ground and merge for mutual longer-term benefits."

"Knock some doors"-

> **Meaning :-** Actively reaching out and making connections with potential business partners or clients.

> **Examples :-**

❖ "John is determined to expand his client base, so he's going to knock some doors and meet with potential customers."

❖ "In order to secure funding for their startup, the team decided to knock some doors and approach venture capitalists."

"Rub shoulders against big boys"-

> **Meaning :-** Engaging with influential individuals for career advancement and business opportunities.

> **Examples :-**

❖ "At the conference, I was rubbing shoulders against big boys to expand my professional network."

❖ "During the industry event, I found myself rubbing shoulders against big boys, discussing potential collaborations and gaining valuable contacts."

"Brownie points"-

> **Meaning :-** Use of personal connections to gain an advantage.

> **Examples :-**

- ❖ "I will use my brownie points to get the CEO to sign off on our proposal."

- ❖ "I will use my brownie points to request a flexible work schedule for next week."

"Political capital"-

> **Meaning :-** Use of political leverage to gain an advantage

> **Examples :-**

- ❖ "I had to use my political capital to secure funding for the project."

- ❖ "The CEO had to use her political capital to rally support among the executives for the company's expansion plans."

"No changes to that ecosystem"-

> **Meaning :-** Maintaining the status quo and not making any changes to a particular system

> **Examples :-**

- ❖ "The IT department decided to make no changes to the current network ecosystem".

- ❖ "The company decided to keep the current management structure with no changes."

"Radio silence"-

> **Meaning :-** No communication or lack of response from someone or a group.

> **Examples :-**

- ❖ "We've been trying to reach the vendor for weeks, but all we're getting is radio silence."

- ❖ "During the project, there was radio silence from the team leader, leaving the team unaware of the progress and next steps."

"Lookie-loo"-

> **Meaning :-** Someone who is curious or interested in something

> **Examples :-**

- ❖ "We had a lot of lookie-loos at the event, but not many actual customers."

- ❖ "During the meeting, John was just a lookie-loo, not contributing anything to the discussion. "

"Ironically pervy"-

> **Meaning:-** Noticing an unexpected and inappropriate behaviour or situation with a touch of irony.

> **Examples :-**

- ❖ "During a team meeting, the CEO's presentation on workplace ethics was ironically pervy as he kept making inappropriate jokes and comments."

- ❖ "The company's strict security measures were ironically pervy when they installed surveillance cameras in the break room, creating an uncomfortable atmosphere for employees."

"Like an owl watching a mouse"-

- ➤ **Meaning :-** You are closely observing someone or something.

- ➤ **Examples :-**

  - ❖ "During the negotiation, the senior executive sat quietly, observing the opposing team, like an owl watching a mouse."

  - ❖ "The manager kept a watchful eye on the new employee's performance, silently observing their every move like an owl watching a mouse."

"Hit closed doors"-

- ➤ **Meaning :-** To face obstacles or resistance.

- ➤ **Examples :-**

  - ❖ "I've been trying to reach out to potential clients, but I am hitting closed doors."

  - ❖ "I am hitting closed doors when it comes to getting promoted despite my hard work and qualifications."

"Stifling environment"-

➢ **Meaning :-** A situation in which progress, creativity, or productivity is hindered or restricted.

➢ **Examples :-**

❖ "In a stifling environment, employees feel discouraged to share innovative ideas, limiting the company's potential for growth and improvement."

❖ "The lack of open communication and micromanagement in a stifling environment leads to low morale and decreased motivation among team members."

"To not ruffle any feathers"-

➢ **Meaning :-** To avoid causing any conflicts or disturbances.

➢ **Examples :-**

❖ "During the team meeting, John carefully chose his words as he presented his ideas, stating, "I don't want to ruffle any feathers, but I think we need to reassess our project timeline.""

❖ "Emily approached her coworker with a concern, prefacing it with, "I don't want to ruffle any feathers, but I noticed some inconsistencies in the financial report that need clarification.""

"Hold or manage the fort"-

> **Meaning:-** To maintain control and responsibility for a particular situation or area of work.

> **Examples :-**

❖ "During the manager's absence, John was asked to hold the fort by overseeing the team's daily operations and ensuring a smooth workflow."

❖ "The CEO had to leave for an urgent meeting, but she trusted her executive assistant to manage the fort and make key decisions in her absence."

"Eyes on the glass"-

> **Meaning :-** Refers to a period of time when close monitoring of a particular situation or process is required, often because of a critical deadline or event.

> **Examples :-**

❖ "We need to keep our eyes on the glass next week to ensure our production schedule stays on track."

❖ "Make sure to keep your eyes on the glass next week to track the progress of our marketing campaign."

"The weekend is young"-

> **Meaning :-** The current time or situation presents a favourable opportunity for action or achievement.

> **Examples :-**

❖ "In a corporate work environment, a team realises they have a few more hours of work left on Friday. They say to each other, "The weekend is young, let's wrap up these tasks and enjoy our time off.""

❖ "During a meeting on Monday morning, a colleague suggests starting a new project. They say, "The weekend is young, let's hit the ground running and make significant progress on this initiative.""

"Overarching theory"-

> **Meaning :-** A guiding principle or concept that encompasses and influences various aspects of a corporate work environment.

> **Examples :-**

❖ "The overarching theory of efficient collaboration promotes clear communication and streamlined processes among team members, leading to improved productivity and better outcomes."

❖ "Embracing the overarching theory of continuous learning fosters a culture of professional development and knowledge-sharing, empowering employees to adapt to new challenges and drive innovation."

"To half-expect something"-

➢ **Meaning** :- To anticipate a certain event or outcome with a sense of caution or skepticism.

➢ **Examples** :-

❖ "During a negotiation, when the opposing party made an unreasonable demand, I half-expected it and was prepared with a counteroffer."

❖ "When a critical deadline was missed due to poor time management, I half-expected it given the team's previous track record."

" Astronomically improbable"-

➢ **Meaning** :- Refers to an event or scenario with an extremely low likelihood of happening.

➢ **Examples** :-

❖ "In a corporate setting, securing a multimillion-dollar deal within a day's notice is astronomically improbable."

❖ "Expecting an intern to single-handedly complete a complex project within an hour is astronomically improbable."

"Gaudy splendor"-

> **Meaning:-** Excessive and flamboyant demonstration or presentation.

> **Examples :-**

❖ "In a corporate event, the CEO arrived at a grand entrance with gaudy splendor, surrounded by extravagant decorations and ostentatious displays."

❖ "The marketing team prepared a product launch with gaudy splendor, incorporating flashy visuals, extravagant giveaways, and an extravagant venue to attract attention and create a memorable experience for attendees."

"Tempest in a tea pot"-

> **Meaning :-** a lot of unnecessary anger and worry about a matter that is not important/something of no importance that causes a great deal of excitement or trouble

> **Examples :-**

❖ "It seemed like an innocent remark, but it set off a tempest in a teapot."

❖ "The disagreement about office supplies turned into a tempest in a teapot, causing unnecessary tension among the team."

"To be snowed"-

> **Meaning :-** Being excessively burdened with tasks or responsibilities.

> **Examples :-**

❖ "We are still snowed with deadlines, and it's causing stress among the team."

❖ "Due to the unexpected influx of projects, we are still snowed with work and need additional resources."

"Chock-a-block"-

> **Meaning :-** Completely packed or full.

> **Examples :-**

❖ "The conference room was chock-a-block with attendees, making it difficult to find a seat."

❖ "The project timeline was chock-a-block with tight deadlines, requiring everyone to work efficiently to meet them."

"Head over heels "-

> **Meaning :-** Being completely engrossed or deeply involved in a particular situation or experience.

- ➤ **Examples :-**
  - ❖ "Sarah was head over heels in a project, working late nights and weekends to ensure its success."
  - ❖ "John fell head over heels for his new role and eagerly took on additional responsibilities to contribute more to the team."

"Pencil In Some Time"-

- ➤ **Meaning :-** Tentatively schedule a meeting or appointment
- ➤ **Examples :-**
  - ❖ "Let's pencil in sometime next week for a follow-up meeting"
  - ❖ "The CEO asked the assistant to pencil in some time for a conference call with investors."

"It is a bit flaky"-

- ➤ **Meaning** :- a person you cannot trust to remember things or to do what they promise, or someone who behaves in a strange way
- ➤ **Examples :-**
  - ❖ "As the story begins, she seems a bit of a flake, and we're not sure how strong her judgment is."
  - ❖ "John's coding skills are valuable, but his attention to detail is a bit flaky."

"Feed forward over feedback"-

> **Meaning** :- Feedforward is the reverse exercise of feedback. It's the process of replacing positive or negative feedback with future-oriented solutions. In simple terms, it means focusing on the future instead of the past.

> **Examples** :-

❖ "During performance reviews, managers focus on providing feedforward by setting clear goals and offering constructive suggestions for improvement."

❖ "In team meetings, members are encouraged to give feedforward by suggesting ideas and solutions to enhance future projects rather than dwelling on past failures."

"It's not my calling"-

> **Meaning** :- Not suited or aligned with one's true purpose or passion.

> **Examples** :-

❖ "When asked to lead a marketing campaign, John declined, saying, It's not my calling. I excel in data analysis and prefer to work on the analytical side of things."

❖ "Sarah turned down a managerial position, explaining, It's not my calling. I thrive in a creative role and find fulfillment in designing and developing innovative solutions."

"Be under the weather"-

> **Meaning:-** Feeling slightly unwell or experiencing a minor setback.

> **Examples :-**

❖ "I am a little under the weather, so I might not be as productive today."

❖ "I am a little under the weather, but I will still attend the meeting and contribute as best as I can."

"To resonate with someone or something"-

> **Meaning :-** To connect or strike a chord with someone on a personal level

> **Examples :-**

❖ "The CEO's speech resonated with me, as I had been through a similar experience."

❖ "The company's mission statement resonated with me, motivating me to give my best at work."

"New age nonsense"-

> **Meaning :-** Modern practices or ideas that are considered impractical or irrelevant in the corporate work environment.

> **Examples :-**

❖ "During an important business meeting, the last thing I need is this new age nonsense in my head, as it can divert my attention from the agenda and key decisions."

❖ "As I strive to meet tight deadlines, the last thing I need is this new age nonsense in my head, as it may disrupt my concentration and impede my progress."

"Your puppet mastery over me ends"-

➢ **Meaning** :- Asserting independence and breaking free from someone's control or manipulation.

➢ **Examples** :-

❖ "In a corporate setting, an employee confronts their micromanaging boss and states, "Your puppet mastery over me ends. I will take ownership of my work and make decisions autonomously.""

❖ "During a team meeting, a junior team member stands up to a dominant colleague and declares, "Your puppet mastery over me ends. I will no longer be overshadowed and will contribute my ideas and opinions confidently.""

"Hole in one's life"-

➢ **Meaning** :- Feeling a lack or void in one's life that affects overall satisfaction and happiness.

> **Examples :-**

> ❖ "Currently there is a hole in my life due to a lack of meaningful relationships and connections at my workplace."

> ❖ "Currently, there is a hole in my life because I haven't found a career that aligns with my passions and interests."

"To not be a small man"-

> ➤ **Meaning :-** A desire to avoid mediocrity or insignificance.

> ➤ **Examples :-**

> ❖ "During team meetings, John actively participates and shares his ideas because he doesn't want to be a small man who remains silent and unnoticed."

> ❖ "Sarah consistently seeks opportunities for skill development and learning new tasks to avoid being a small man confined to a narrow skill set."

"To not dwell on one's misfortunes"-

> ➤ **Meaning :-** Focus on self-improvement rather than dwelling on past setbacks.

> ➤ **Examples :-**

> ❖ "In a corporate setting, instead of fixating on a failed project, focus on learning from it and developing new skills."

❖ "When facing a setback at work, don't dwell on the misfortune, but rather embrace it as an opportunity for personal growth and resilience."

"It doesn't tickle my fancy"-

➤ **Meaning :-** It doesn't appeal to me or suit my taste.

➤ **Examples :-**

❖ "The new office design proposal doesn't tickle my fancy; I prefer a more minimalist approach."

❖ "I appreciate the effort, but the team-building activity suggested doesn't tickle my fancy; I'd rather engage in a community service project instead."

"Affinity for numbers"-

➤ **Meaning :-** A natural liking or inclination towards working with numbers

➤ **Examples :-**

❖ "The finance team must have an affinity for numbers to be able to analyse financial data and create reports."

❖ "A successful data analyst has a strong affinity for numbers and can interpret complex data sets with ease."

"Other side of the coin"-

> ➤ **Meaning :-** Referring to an alternative viewpoint or perspective on a topic

> ➤ **Examples :-**

> ❖ "While we have considered the pros, we also need to look at the other side of the coin."

> ❖ "Implementing cost-cutting measures may boost short-term profitability, but the other side of the coin is the potential negative impact on employee morale and productivity."

"To talk someone out "-

> ➤ **Meaning :-** To make an effort to dissuade someone from their chosen course of action.

> ➤ **Examples :-**

> ❖ "During the project meeting, you didn't even try to talk him out of it when he proposed an inefficient approach."

> ❖ "Despite knowing the risks involved, you didn't even try to talk him out of it when he decided to invest in that dubious venture."

"Silver-tongued devil"-

> ➤ **Meaning :-** A highly skilled communicator who uses their charm and eloquence to influence others.

> **Examples :-**

- ❖ "During the sales presentation, John effortlessly persuaded the client to sign the contract, showcasing why he truly is the silver-tongued devil."

- ❖ "In the boardroom, Sarah's persuasive abilities were on full display as she successfully convinced her colleagues to adopt her innovative marketing strategy, earning her the title of the silver-tongued devil."

"Finger in the air estimate"-

> **Meaning :-** A method of doing something that is not scientific or accurate

> **Examples :-**

- ❖ "During the meeting, the team gave a finger in the air estimate of the project budget without considering all the variables."

- ❖ "The project manager provided a finger in the air estimate for the completion date based on initial requirements."

"To stack someone"-

> **Meaning :-** To manipulate or influence a group or organisation in one's favour

> **Examples :-**

- ❖ "The senator was accused of trying to stack congress to get his bill passed"

❖ "He stacked congress by strategically placing his allies in key positions of power, ensuring favourable outcomes for his policies."

"It would definitely be the high point of my day"-

➢ **Meaning:-** The event or scenario that would bring the most satisfaction or happiness during the day.

➢ **Examples:-**

❖ "Receiving recognition for a successful project presentation would definitely be the high point of my day."

❖ "Closing a significant deal with a client would definitely be the high point of my day."

"Not the end of the world"-

➢ **Meaning :-** Things are not as bad as they may seem

➢ **Examples :-**

❖ "We missed the deadline, but it's not the end of the world. Let's regroup and come up with a plan."

❖ "The client rejected our proposal, but it is not the end of the world. We can learn from their feedback and refine our approach."

"Purple patch"-

> **Meaning** :- A period of time when everything is going well or when a person is performing exceptionally well

> **Examples** :-

❖ "Our team has been on a purple patch lately, winning the last five games in a row."

❖ "The company is going through a purple patch, with revenues increasing significantly in the last quarter."

"To be dead in water"-

> **Meaning** :- To have hope and not give up despite setbacks

> **Examples** :-

❖ "We had a few setbacks, but we are not dead in the water yet."

❖ "Despite initial setbacks, we implemented a new strategy and now we're not dead in the water."

"Let's pin that for now"-

> **Meaning** :- Temporarily postpone a discussion or decision for later

> **Examples** :-

- ❖ "Let's pin that for now and discuss it at our next meeting when we have more information."

- ❖ "During the meeting, one team member suggested a new project idea, but the team agreed to pin that for now and focus on the current project's completion first."

"To table something"-

> **Meaning** :- To postpone or set aside a topic or issue for future discussion or consideration.

> **Examples** :-

- ❖ "During the meeting, John suggested a new marketing strategy, but due to time constraints, the team decided to table it for some other time."

- ❖ "The management committee encountered a contentious issue, so they agreed to table it for some other time to allow for further research and analysis."

"Corporate imperialism"-

> **Meaning** :- The dominance of a corporation over other entities, exerting control and influence.

> **Examples :-**

> ❖ "The CEO's decisions reflected a form of corporate imperialism, where dissenting opinions were ignored or silenced."

> ❖ "The company's aggressive expansion strategy displayed elements of corporate imperialism, as it aimed to control markets and eliminate competition."

"Proving prophetic"-

> **Meaning :-** A situation where a prediction or foresight about a decision turns out to be accurate.

> **Examples :-**

> ❖ "The account gives the reader some idea of what is taking place in the context of prophetic vision"

> ❖ "The team's hesitance to implement a new software system proved prophetic as it caused major technical issues."

"To line up one's ducks"-

> **Meaning :-** to be well prepared or well organised for something that is going to happen:

> **Examples :-**

> ❖ "They should have had their ducks in a row beforehand, so they were ready to start the job when required."

❖ "The team had a flawless presentation because they knew how their ducks were lined up."

"To do very old razzle-dazzle"-

➤ Meaning:- To deliver an impressive and captivating presentation.

➤ **Examples :-**

   ❖ "During the conference, I did the very old razzle-dazzle and received a standing ovation for my presentation on market trends."

   ❖ I did the very old razzle-dazzle in the boardroom by incorporating interactive visuals and engaging storytelling to win the client's approval for our proposal."

"Put One On The Spot"-

➤ **Meaning** :- To ask someone a difficult question or request, often in a public setting

➤ **Examples :-**

   ❖ "During the Q&A session, the CEO put the speaker on the spot with a challenging question."

   ❖ "The presentation unexpectedly went off track, putting the speaker on the spot to handle tough questions from the audience."

"Push one into a corner"-

> **Meaning** :- The use of force or coercion to achieve a desired outcome

> **Examples** :-

  ❖ "We cannot resort to pushing our employees into a corner to get the work done."

  ❖ "In a high-stakes project, the team leader is pushing him into a corner to get the work done before the deadline."

"Bigger fish to fry"-

> **Meaning** :- To not be interested in something because you have more important, interesting, or profitable things to do.

> **Examples** :-

  ❖ "I can't worry about that now, I've got bigger fish to fry"

  ❖ "She couldn't finish the report on time because she had a bigger fish to fry with the urgent client request."

"Most pressing issue at hand"-

> **Meaning** :- The crucial task of making choices or reaching conclusions in a timely manner.

> ➢ **Examples :-**

  ❖ "In our team meeting, the most pressing issue at hand is decision-making regarding the new product launch strategy."

  ❖ "With multiple deadlines approaching, the team must collectively identify the most pressing issue at hand to allocate resources effectively."

"Open-ended exploration"-

➢ **Meaning:-** Begin with an open-ended investigation, and confirm the existence of a problem later.

➢ **Examples :-**

  ❖ "In a project, you can begin by exploring various possibilities and later verify if there is an actual problem that needs to be addressed."

  ❖ "When troubleshooting an issue at work, it's effective to start with an open-ended exploration to gather information and then validate the problem before devising a solution."

"Go back to the first principles"-

➢ **Meaning :-** Asking to revisit the basic principles or assumptions underlying a problem in order to come up with a more effective solution

> **Examples :-**

❖ "We've tried a lot of different strategies for marketing this product, but nothing seems to be working. Can we go back to the first principles and rethink our target audience?"

❖ "During the board meeting, the CEO asked, Can we go back to the first principles and reevaluate our long-term growth strategy?"

"Last Piece Of The Puzzle"-

> **Meaning :-** The final element or solution needed to complete a task or resolve an issue.

> **Examples :-**

❖ "John's innovative idea was the last piece of the puzzle that allowed the team to successfully launch the new product."

❖ "After months of research and collaboration, the market analysis report became the last piece of the puzzle, enabling the company to make informed strategic decisions."

"To Move The Needle"-

> **Meaning :-** To make significant progress or achieve desired outcomes?

> **Examples :-**

❖ "We need to move the needle on global poverty. "

❖ "During a project review meeting, a team leader asks, So how do you move the needle? to encourage brainstorming and find innovative solutions to overcome challenges."

"Needle In A Haystack"-

➢ **Meaning** :- someone or something that is very hard to find

➢ **Examples** :-

❖ "Searching for your earring at the park will be like looking for a needle in a haystack."

❖ "Finding a cost-effective solution for our company's budget constraints is like looking for a needle in a haystack."

"To Digest Information"-

➢ **Meaning** :- The process of comprehending and assimilating information.

➢ **Examples** :-

❖ "He will take the time to carefully digest this information, thoroughly analyse it, and then come back with a well-considered and thought-out solution or response."

❖ "During the board meeting, the CEO stated, He is going to digest this information and come back to indicate that further consideration was needed before making a final decision on the proposed merger."

"To Go Back To The Well"-

> **Meaning** :- Return to a previously successful method or approach.

> **Examples** :-

❖ "Our marketing campaign didn't yield the desired results. Let's go back to the well and use the strategy that worked for us before."

❖ "The new software update has caused glitches in our system. We should go back to the well and revert to the previous version that was stable."

"To Vector An Issue"-

> **Meaning** :- Continuously addressing and directing attention towards resolving an issue.

> **Examples** :-

❖ "In a team meeting, despite previous discussions, the team is still vectoring the issue of poor customer feedback, aiming to find a solution and improve customer satisfaction."

❖ "The project manager noticed a recurring problem with delayed deliverables and mentioned, We are still vectoring the issue of missed deadlines and exploring ways to enhance our project timeline management."

"To Rack One's Brain"-

> ➤ **Meaning :-** Engaging in intense mental effort to find a solution or answer.

> ➤ **Examples :-**

>> ❖ "I am racking my brain to come up with a creative solution to this project challenge."

>> ❖ "I am racking my brain trying to figure out the best strategy to improve our sales numbers."

"To Get Genie Back In The Bottle"-

> ➤ **Meaning :-** Addressing and resolving a difficult situation or issue.

> ➤ **Examples :-**

>> ❖ "In a project that has gone off track, the team realises they need to get this genie back in the bottle by revisiting the initial objectives and implementing corrective measures."

>> ❖ "After a breach of confidential information, the company acknowledges the need to get this genie back in the bottle by strengthening security measures and regaining control over sensitive data."

"Pressure-Test One's Solution"-

> ➤ **Meaning :-** Assessing the effectiveness and resilience of a proposed solution through rigorous testing.

> **Examples :-**

❖ "During the project review, I wanna pressure-test my solution to identify any weaknesses or vulnerabilities before implementation."

❖ "In order to ensure the reliability of our new software, I wanna pressure-test my solution by simulating various scenarios and stress conditions."

"Leave No Stone Unturned"-

> **Meaning** :-Exhaustive effort to explore all possible avenues for a solution.

> **Examples :-**

❖ "When faced with a challenging project, the team left no stone unturned in researching and analysing every aspect before presenting their findings."

❖ "The company's audit team left no stone unturned in reviewing financial records to ensure accuracy and compliance with regulations."

"In No Mood For Riddles"-

> **Meaning** :- Lack of tolerance for unnecessary complications or unclear explanations during the problem-solving process.

> **Examples :-**

❖ "In a team brainstorming session, one member exclaimed, I am in no mood for riddles. Let's stick to straightforward solutions and address the problem at hand."

❖ "The CEO addressed the team, saying, I am in no mood for riddles when it comes to our company's future. Give me clear facts and figures to support your proposals."

"Grease The Wheels"-

> **Meaning :-** A statement that suggests one has the ability to make things happen quickly

> **Examples :-**

❖ "The project manager said to the team, If we need to expedite the timeline, I can grease the wheels really fast if I want to."

❖ "In a high-pressure negotiation, I can grease the wheels really fast if I want to and secure a favourable deal for our company."

"Snapping Turtle"-

> **Meaning :-** A difficult or challenging situation that requires immediate attention and resolution.

> **Examples :-**

❖ "In a high-pressure board meeting, the CEO acted like a snapping turtle, swiftly making tough decisions to navigate the company through the crisis."

❖ "The project team faced a snapping turtle situation when a critical deadline was unexpectedly moved up, forcing them to rapidly reorganise their tasks and priorities."

"Know The Drill"-

➤ **Meaning** :- To be familiar with a process or routine that is regularly followed

➤ **Examples** :-

❖ "A new employee being told Once you know the drill, it will be easy to complete this task"

❖ "Before the project starts, make sure everyone knows the drill for submitting their weekly progress reports."

"Busy Beaver"-

➤ **Meaning** :- Someone who is consistently and diligently working on tasks or projects.

➤ **Examples** :-

❖ "John is a busy beaver, always focused and dedicated to completing his assignments on time."

❖ "The team's busy beaver, Sarah, single-handedly managed to finish the project ahead of schedule due to her relentless work ethic."

"Arm Candy"-

> **Meaning** :- The use of an attractive or visually appealing person to enhance one's professional image or presence.

> **Examples** :-

❖ "In corporate events, executives often bring arm candy to project a successful and influential image."

❖ "Some individuals rely on arm candy during important business meetings to create a positive first impression and establish credibility."

"No Shop Talk"-

> **Meaning** :- Avoiding work-related discussions in a specific context.

> **Examples:** -

❖ "During a team lunch, everyone agrees to abide by the rule of No shop talk to ensure a relaxed and non-work-focused atmosphere."

❖ "At a company social event, employees are reminded with a friendly notice to keep conversations light-hearted and refrain from engaging in any work-related discussions. No shop talk is the golden rule for the evening."

"I Am Sorry To Interrupt You During Your Downtime"-

> ➤ **Meaning** :- Expressing regret for interrupting someone during their personal time or designated break.

> ➤ **Examples** :-

>> ❖ "I am sorry to interrupt you during your downtime, but there's an urgent matter that requires your attention."

>> ❖ "I am sorry to interrupt you during your downtime, but there's a client on the line who needs immediate assistance."

"Move Leaps And Bounds"-

> ➤ **Meaning** :-Move forward in surprisingly large and rapid steps.

> ➤ **Examples** :-

>> ❖ "Our marketing campaign is moving leaps and bounds, attracting double the expected number of customers."

>> ❖ "The company's revenue is growing exponentially, moving leaps and bounds ahead of our competitors."

"To Have An Anchor Hanging Up"-

> ➤ **Meaning** :- There is a hindrance or obstacle affecting your progress or success.

- ➤ **Examples :-**
  - ❖ "You got an anchor hanging up, it's slowing down the completion of the project."
  - ❖ "His lack of attention to detail is an anchor hanging up on our team's progress."

"My Dancing Will End Here"-

- ➤ **Meaning** :- The assessment of one's performance or development in a given situation.

- ➤ **Examples :-**
  - ❖ "During my annual performance review, I told my manager, My dancing will end here, indicating that I have reached my peak performance and need new challenges."
  - ❖ "In a team meeting discussing project updates, I confidently stated, My dancing will end here, implying that I have completed my assigned tasks and now require additional responsibilities."

"Light At End Of The Tunnel"-

- ➤ **Meaning** :- a reason to believe that a bad situation will end soon or that a long and difficult job will be finished soon

- ➤ **Examples :-**
  - ❖ "Despite facing numerous setbacks, the team saw the light at the end of the tunnel as they

approached the completion of a major project."

* ❖ "he company's financial struggles were alleviated when they discovered the light at the end of the tunnel through a successful investment opportunity."

"Safe, Secure And Sound Manner"-

> **Meaning** :- Launching a project in a secure manner

> **Examples :-**

* ❖ "We need to ensure that we go live in a safe secure and sound way"

* ❖ "The IT team is working diligently to ensure the product deployment goes live in a safe, secure, and sound way, adhering to all quality standards and protocols."

"On the run up to go live"-

> **Meaning** :-We are in the preparation phase leading up to the official launch.

> **Examples :-**

* ❖ "We are on the run-up to going live, so everyone needs to double-check their tasks and ensure everything is ready for the project launch."

* ❖ "As we are on the run-up to going live, it's crucial that we maintain clear communication

among team members to address any last-minute issues before the launch."

"Utopian Greenfield Outcome"-

> **Meaning** :- A desired and ideal outcome for a new project or initiative

> **Examples** :-

  ❖ "The project team had a utopian Greenfield outcome in mind for the new software development project"

  ❖ "The company had a utopian Greenfield outcome for the acquisition of a new company."

"To Get Something Underway"-

> **Meaning** :- To start or begin a process or project

> **Examples** :-

  ❖ "We need to get this testing under way before the deadline."

  ❖ "The success of our project depends on efficient testing, so we need to get this testing under way promptly."

"Further Down In Waterfall"-

> **Meaning** :- A reference to the later stages of a project, often used in the context of software development projects using the waterfall methodology

> **Examples :-**

❖ "We're still in the early stages of development. We'll address that issue further down in the waterfall."

❖ "As we move further down in the waterfall, the development team starts coding based on the finalised requirements."

"Gold Plating"-

➢ **Meaning** :- Adding unnecessary or excessive features to a project, which can lead to delays or increased costs

➢ **Examples :-**

❖ "We need to avoid gold plating the project and focus on delivering what the client actually needs."

❖ "The development team engaged in gold plating by adding fancy animations to the website, even though it wasn't part of the client's specifications."

"To Bottom Out Something"-

➢ **Meaning** :- To reach the lowest point or to resolve all the issues in a project

➢ **Examples :-**

❖ "After months of debugging, we finally bottomed that out."

❖ "We bottomed that out by cutting unnecessary expenses and optimising resource allocation."

"To Approach End Of The Road"-

➢ **Meaning** :- Reaching the end of a project or an option

➢ **Examples :-**

❖ "We need to find a solution quickly; we are approaching the end of the road."

❖ "As the company was approaching the end of the road with its outdated technology, a transition period was initiated to adopt new systems."

"Fluid Requirements"-

➢ **Meaning** :- The expectation that project requirements may change during the development cycle

➢ **Examples :-**

❖ "We need to be flexible as requirements are fluid and may change during development."

❖ "During the development process, stakeholders may provide new inputs or modify their preferences, leading to fluid requirements that need to be adjusted accordingly."

"Until The Cow's Home"-

> **Meaning** :- for a very long time

> **Examples** :-

  ❖ "I could sit here and argue with you till the cows come home, but it wouldn't solve anything."

  ❖ "You can dream until the cow's home, but unless we take action, our team won't achieve the desired outcomes."

"Stonewall Someone Or Something"-

> **Meaning** :- Willfully withholding information or avoiding communication with the press.

> **Examples** :-

  ❖ "In a corporate crisis, the CEO said, I don't mind stonewalling the press to maintain control over the narrative and limit media access to sensitive information."

  ❖ "During a product launch, the marketing team decided, I don't mind stonewalling the press to keep key features and surprises hidden until the official announcement."

"Reject Every Bit of Rat And Mice"-

> **Meaning** :- Rejecting substandard or faulty components.

> Examples :-

* ❖ "I don't want every bit of rat and mice in our production line; we need to ensure strict quality control measures to maintain high standards."

* ❖ "We should avoid accepting every bit of rat and mice in our suppliers' deliveries to prevent any compromised product quality."

"Instinctive Response"-

> **Meaning** :- Immediate, intuitive reaction or action taken without conscious deliberation.

> Examples :-

* ❖ "In a high-pressure situation, his instinctive response was to trust his gut and make a quick decision."

* ❖ "When faced with ambiguity, her instinctive response was to gather more information before taking any action."

"To Sing For One's Supper"-

> **Meaning** :- to do something for someone else in order to receive something in return,

> Examples :-

* ❖ "The cruise lecturers are academics singing for their supper."

* ❖ "In a sales pitch, a representative says, I'll sing for my supper, I don't get it for me, implying

their willingness to go the extra mile to secure the client's business in exchange for a commission or financial reward."

"To Recover One's Wits"-

> **Meaning** :- Regaining composure and clarity of mind to make sound decisions.

> **Examples** :-

❖ "In the midst of a high-pressure negotiation, take a brief break to regain your composure. You can recover your wits and make well-informed choices."

❖ "When faced with a sudden workplace crisis, step back, breathe, and assess the situation calmly. You can recover your wits and make effective decisions to address the issue."

"Chew the cuds"-

> **Meaning** :-Engage in thoughtful analysis or introspection.

> **Examples** :-

❖ "During the team meeting, we need to chew the cuds to evaluate our progress and identify areas for improvement."

❖ "Before making any important decisions, it's crucial to chew the cuds individually and then come together to discuss our thoughts and insights."

"Won't Risk Everything For A Roll In The Hay"-

> ➤ **Meaning** :- Refusing to jeopardise everything for a momentary pleasure or short-term gain.

> ➤ **Examples** :-

> ❖ "When considering a business partnership, I won't risk everything for a roll in the hay; I'll prioritise long-term sustainability and reliability."

> ❖ "As a manager, I won't risk everything for a roll in the hay by compromising team integrity for personal interests; I'll prioritise ethical behaviour and professionalism."

"Object Of Ridicule"-

> ➤ **Meaning** :- If someone or something is an object of ridicule or is held up to ridicule, someone makes fun of them in an unkind way.

> ➤ **Examples** :-

> ❖ "Due to his inappropriate remarks during a team meeting, he has become the object of ridicule among his colleagues."

> ❖ "His consistent failure to meet project deadlines has led to him being the object of ridicule among the project team."

"Humor Me"-

> ➤ **Meaning** :- To request someone to indulge or humour the speaker's request or idea, usually in a lighthearted or joking manner

> ➤ **Examples** :-

>> ❖ "Humor me for a second, but what if we changed the logo to pink and green?"

>> ❖ "I know it sounds crazy, but just humour me on this and let's try it out."

"Fight An Uphill Battle"-

> ➤ **Meaning** :- Facing significant challenges or obstacles while trying to achieve a desired outcome.

> ➤ **Examples** :-

>> ❖ "In implementing a new company-wide policy, we are fighting an uphill battle to gain employee buy-in and change their established habits."

>> ❖ "With a limited budget and tight deadlines, we are fighting an uphill battle to deliver a high-quality product that meets customer expectations."

"Stick In The Mud"-

> ➤ **Meaning** :- Someone who is unwilling to adapt or embrace new ideas or methods.

> ➤ **Examples** :-

- ❖ "In the team meeting, John was a stick in the mud, refusing to consider any suggestions for improving the project's workflow."

- ❖ "Despite the need for innovation, the company's outdated policies and procedures created a stick-in-the-mud culture that hindered progress."

"It Wouldn't Soften My Resolve"-

> ➤ **Meaning** :- A phrase used to convey that a person's decision or stance cannot be altered by external factors

> ➤ **Examples** :-

- ❖ "The competitor's offer was tempting, but it wouldn't soften my resolve to stick with our company's values."

- ❖ "Even if there's opposition from colleagues, it wouldn't soften my resolve to pursue innovative ideas."

"Water Under The Bridge"-

> ➤ **Meaning** :- Past issues that no longer have an impact or are no longer worth dwelling upon.

> ➤ **Examples** :-

- ❖ "We had a disagreement about the project, but let's consider it water under the bridge and focus on moving forward."

❖ "John made a mistake in the presentation, but we'll let it be water under the bridge and not hold it against him."

"To Use A Rolls Royce For Something That Can Be Done by Volkswagen"-

➤ **Meaning** :- Avoiding the use of high-cost resources for tasks that can be accomplished with more economical alternatives.

➤ **Examples** :-

❖ "When planning projects, we should avoid assigning senior executives to routine administrative tasks. We don't want to use a Rolls Royce for something that can be done by Volkswagen."

❖ "Instead of hiring expensive consultants for minor research tasks, let's utilise our in-house team. We don't want to use a Rolls Royce for something that can be done by Volkswagen."

"A Cook Cannot Blame His Ingredients"-

➤ **Meaning** :- To take ownership of one's actions and not blame external factors

➤ **Examples** :-

❖ "The project manager told his team that they can't blame the tools or software for their mistakes, because a cook cannot blame his ingredients"

❖ "During a performance review, a manager reminds an employee about the significance of taking ownership by saying, "Remember, a cook cannot blame his ingredients. Take responsibility for your decisions and actions to achieve better results.""

"Poke The Bear"-

➢ **Meaning** :- To avoid taking unnecessary risks or upsetting a situation

➢ **Examples** :-

❖ "The team decided not to implement the controversial feature because they didn't want to go poking the bear so much."

❖ "The manager warned the team not to go poking the bear so much by engaging in untested strategies."

"Don't See Any Landmines"-

➢ **Meaning** :- Not seeing any potential issues or obstacles

➢ **Examples** :-

❖ "After reviewing the proposal, I don't see any landmines that could hinder its success."

❖ "When discussing a new business venture, the CEO confidently states, I don't see any landmines in this plan."

"Bait The Hook, See If One Bites"-

> **Meaning:-** Test someone's reaction or vulnerability to potential risks.

> **Examples :-**

❖ "In a security audit, the IT department sets up a simulated phishing email to bait the hook and see if any employees fall for it."

❖ "A project manager intentionally presents a controversial idea during a team meeting to bait the hook and gauge the team's response and potential risks involved."

"Neutralise The Threat"-

> **Meaning :-** Reducing or eliminating the potential harm or danger

> **Examples :-**

❖ "The company implemented new security measures to neutralise the threat of cyber attacks."

❖ "By implementing strict security measures, we neutralised the threat of unauthorised access to sensitive data."

"To Not Get Caught Out"-

> **Meaning :-** Avoiding unforeseen risks or challenges

> **Examples :-**

❖ "Let's make sure we have a contingency plan; we don't want to get caught out."

❖ "Before launching a new product, we thoroughly test it to ensure we don't want to get caught out by any potential defects or issues."

"To Dodge A Bullet"-

> **Meaning** :- to escape an uncomfortable situation, or to have successfully avoided a serious problem'

> **Examples :-**

❖ "I really dodged the bullet when my exam was postponed to next week, as I hadn't studied for it at all!"

❖ "After extensive testing, we discovered a critical flaw in the software just before release. We just dodged a bullet by fixing it in time."

"To go into a dark hole"-

> **Meaning** :- If you say that something, especially money, has gone into a black hole, you mean that it has disappeared and cannot be recovered.

> **Examples :-**

❖ "Concerned we are going into a dark hole without assessing the potential risks and establishing contingency plans."

❖ "The team is concerned we are going into a dark hole by investing heavily in a new market without proper risk management measures in place."

"To Throw Oneself In The Harm's Way"-

> **Meaning** :- To expose oneself to potential harm or danger.

> **Examples :-**

❖ "During a project, don't take unnecessary risks that could jeopardise the team's progress or safety. Don't throw yourselves in harm's way."

❖ "When faced with a potentially dangerous client situation, prioritise safety and caution over personal ambition. Don't throw yourselves in harm's way."

"To Test The Waters"-

> **Meaning** :- To try something new or unfamiliar to see if it's feasible or worth pursuing further

> **Examples :-**

❖ "Let's just test the waters and see if this marketing campaign is effective before investing more resources"

❖ "Before launching a new product, the marketing team decided to just test the waters by running a limited market research campaign to gather initial feedback from potential customers."

"Same Gig As Always"-

➢ **Meaning :-** The repetition of familiar tasks or responsibilities.

➢ **Examples :-**

❖ "We're stuck in the same gig as always, just processing paperwork day after day."

❖ "The team meeting turned out to be the same gig as always, discussing the same old topics with no new insights."

"Word On The Street"-

➢ **Meaning :-** Information or gossip that is circulating

➢ **Examples :-**

❖ "The word on the street is that the company is planning to lay off employees in the next quarter."

❖ "The word on the street is that the CEO is stepping down."

"Sell Ice To The Eskimos"-

➢ **Meaning** :-Refers to someone who is very persuasive and can sell anything

➢ **Examples** :-

❖ "We need him on our sales team, he can sell ice to Eskimos."

❖ "He can sell ice to Eskimos - He has exceptional negotiation skills and can find common ground even in the most challenging conflicts."

"To Sell Cats To Mice"-

➢ **Meaning** :- An individual who can persuade people into buying something, even if it is not necessary

➢ **Examples** :-

❖ "He has a talent for selling and can convince anyone to buy anything."

❖ "Despite the challenging market conditions, his persuasive skills were so strong that he could sell cats to mice and close deals effortlessly."

"Weed Out"-

➢ **Meaning** :- To eliminate unsuitable candidates or options

> ➤ Examples :-

> ❖ "Our hiring process really weeds out the bad candidates from the good ones."

> ❖ "By implementing thorough background checks, the organisation can weed out the bad guys and maintain a safe and trustworthy work environment."

"To Be Jolted Back Into Reality"-

> ➤ **Meaning** :- To recognize the need for a reality check or a wake-up call

> ➤ **Examples** :-

> ❖ "After getting lost in his work, he realised he needed to be jolted back into reality sometimes"

> ❖ "When I spend too much time daydreaming or procrastinating at work, my supervisor gives me a stern reminder, jolting me back into reality and urging me to focus on my tasks and deadlines."

"To Cut Oneself Some Slack"-

> ➤ **Meaning** :- Give yourself a break or be less critical of yourself.

> ➤ **Examples** :-

> ❖ "After a long and demanding project, the team should cut themselves some slack and

celebrate their achievements before diving into the next task."

❖ "During performance evaluations, managers should remind employees to cut themselves some slack and not be too hard on themselves for minor mistakes."

"Don't Be Too Hard On Oneself"-

➢ **Meaning** :- Avoid being excessively critical of your own actions or performance.

➢ **Examples** :-

❖ "After a presentation, a team member is disappointed with their delivery and starts berating themselves. A colleague consoles them, saying, Don't be too hard on yourself. You did a great job overall."

❖ "An employee makes a minor mistake in a report and becomes upset. The manager reassures them, saying, It's just a small error. Don't be too hard on yourself. We all make mistakes sometimes."

"Sensitized To It"-

➢ **Meaning** :- Aware of a situation and its nuances

➢ **Examples** :-

❖ "We need to be sensitised to the cultural differences when we are negotiating with our international partners."

❖ "The company conducted cybersecurity training to sensitise employees to the risks associated with phishing attacks and data breaches."

"To Strike A Nerve"-

➢ **Meaning :-** Questioning if a comment or action has caused an emotional reaction or offence.

➢ **Examples :-**

❖ "During a team meeting, a colleague makes a suggestion that challenges the expertise of another team member. The person responds defensively, and the colleague asks, Did my lump of clay remark strike a nerve?"

❖ "In a performance review, a manager criticises an employee's work quality. The employee becomes defensive and responds, Did my lump of clay remark strike a nerve?"

"Handle Touchy Subjects With Kid Gloves"-

➢ **Meaning :-** Approach delicate or sensitive topics with caution and tact.

➢ **Examples :-**

❖ "In a corporate meeting, it's important to handle touchy subjects with kid gloves to avoid offending anyone and maintain a respectful and productive environment."

* ❖ "When providing feedback on a colleague's performance issue, it's crucial to handle touchy subjects with kid gloves to ensure open communication and preserve professional relationships."

"Cut From The Same Cloth"-

➤ **Meaning** :- Having a similar approach or mindset when making choices.

➤ **Examples** :-

* ❖ "Don't assume all women are cut from the same cloth."

* ❖ "Our team members always agree on project priorities - we are cut from the same cloth."

"Tenuous Theory"-

➤ **Meaning** :- A doubtful or uncertain idea that lacks credibility

➤ **Examples** :-

* ❖ "The theory that the earth is flat is tenuous and not supported by scientific evidence."

* ❖ "The executive review committee dismissed the proposal, stating, That is a pretty tenuous theory; it lacks the necessary scientific backing for us to invest in it."

"To Develop New Muscles"-

> **Meaning** :- The process of acquiring new skills and abilities.

> **Examples** :-

❖ "Developing new muscles in adaptability by quickly learning and using new software tools."

❖ "Developing new muscles in time management by using productivity tools and techniques to maximise work efficiency."

"To Be Out Of Someone's League"-

> **Meaning** :- Not at a level where one is as good as someone else at something

> **Examples** :-

❖ "Am sorry that's out of my league, I don't have the technical knowledge to troubleshoot the software issue."

❖ "Am sorry that's out of my league, I'm not trained in financial analysis to provide accurate investment advice."

"Progress Reduced To A Crawl"-

> **Meaning** :- Progress that is very slow or almost non-existent

> **Examples :-**

❖ "Despite our best efforts, progress on the project has reduced to a crawl in the last few months."

❖ "Due to various challenges and setbacks, progress in the last few months reduced to a crawl, resulting in missed deadlines and a backlog of tasks."

"To Rain On Someone's Celebrations"-

> **Meaning :-** To spoil someone's joyful occasion or achievement.

> **Examples :-**

❖ "At the office party, I really didn't want to rain on her celebrations by pointing out the mistakes in her presentation."

❖ "After our team won the project bid, I really didn't want to rain on her celebrations by reminding everyone of the impending tight deadline for completion."

"It's No Silver Bullet"-

> **Meaning :-** A solution that will not completely solve the problem

> **Examples :-**

❖ "We need to diversify our revenue streams. Lowering prices is no silver bullet."

❖ "Implementing new software can improve efficiency, but it's no silver bullet for all productivity issues."

"Cherry-Pick Someone Or Something"-

➢ **Meaning** :- To choose the best ones from a group of them, often in a way that other people consider unfair.

➢ **Examples** :-

❖ "The success of our marketing campaign depends on cherry-picking a few people who have a deep understanding of our target audience."

❖ "In order to form an effective project team, we need to cherry-pick a few people with the right expertise and skills."

"Where Did This Land"-

➢ **Meaning** :- The status or outcome of a situation

➢ **Examples** :-

❖ "I'm not sure where we stand with the contract. Where did this land?"

❖ "After implementing the new marketing strategy, where did this land in terms of customer engagement and sales?"

"To Pivot"-

> **Meaning** :-To shift or change direction in response to a new situation or data

> **Examples :-**

❖ "The company decided to pivot after that and focus on a new market opportunity."

❖ "The team decided to pivot after that and switch to a more agile approach."

"Play The Long Game"-

> **Meaning** :- A long-term plan or approach to achieve a desired outcome

> **Examples :-**

❖ "We need to consider playing the long game to achieve sustainable growth."

❖ "I am playing the long game by carefully building relationships with potential clients, knowing that it may take time to secure their business."

"Whittled down to the bone"-

> **Meaning** :- Reducing something to its essential elements or eliminating unnecessary aspects.

> **Examples :-**

❖ "The project budget was whittled down to the bone to maximise cost efficiency and meet financial targets."

* ❖ "After several rounds of revisions, the proposal was whittled down to the bone to focus on the key deliverables and eliminate any extraneous information."

"To Wear Down One's Nerves"-

- ➢ **Meaning** :- Feeling overwhelmed or irritated due to work-related factors.

- ➢ **Examples** :-

    - ❖ "The constant pressure and unrealistic deadlines are wearing down my nerves."

    - ❖ "The lack of communication and disorganised workflow is wearing down my nerves."

"To Stick Out One's Neck"-

- ➢ **Meaning** :- To take a bold or risky action, often in a challenging or uncertain situation.

- ➢ **Examples** :-

    - ❖ "Despite my efforts, my colleague refuses to support my proposal during the team meeting. He is not going to stick his neck out for me."

    - ❖ "I made a mistake at work, and when I asked my supervisor for assistance, he showed no interest in helping me. He is not going to stick his neck out for me."

"Get someone's back"-

> **Meaning** :- To offer support and protection to someone in need

> **Examples** :-

* ❖ "The team leader assured the new employee that she had their back if they needed any help."

* ❖ "The security team implemented strict measures to ensure data protection, showing that they've got our back when it comes to safeguarding sensitive information."

"Shuck a bag of corn"-

> **Meaning** :- A task that requires a lot of effort or work to complete

> **Examples** :-

* ❖ "The project is a bag of corn that needs to be shucked, but we'll get it done."

* ❖ "The urgent client request is like a bag of corn that needs to be shucked; we must prioritise and handle it promptly."

"To wipe off the table"-

> **Meaning** :- To finish or complete a task or assignment.

> **Examples :-**

❖ "After the team meeting, they started wiping off the table by finalising the project plan and assigning tasks."

❖ "The manager wiped off the table by reviewing and approving all pending reports before the deadline."

"To get cracking"-

> **Meaning :-** act quickly and decisively.

> **Examples :-**

❖ "most tickets have been snapped up, so get cracking if you want one "

❖ "Before a work presentation, a colleague says, We need to impress the clients. Let's get cracking and rehearse our pitch until it's perfect."

"Maintain the operating rhythm"-

> **Meaning :-** Ensuring consistent progress and adherence to established procedures.

> **Examples :-**

❖ "To maintain the operating rhythm, employees must complete tasks within the given timeframes and follow established workflows."

❖ "In order to maintain the operating rhythm, the team needs to prioritise tasks effectively and keep a steady pace to achieve their goals."

"To look like a dog's breakfast"-

➢ **Meaning** :- The situation is disorganised or chaotic.

➢ **Examples** :-

❖ "During the project review meeting, the team's presentation materials were scattered, inconsistent, and poorly prepared. It looked like a dog's breakfast."

❖ "The company's filing system was a mess, with documents misplaced and folders mislabeled. Trying to find important files was like searching through a dog's breakfast."

"You don't tie a bundle of wood with one hand"-

➢ **Meaning** :- Completing a complex task or achieving a goal requires sufficient effort and resources.

➢ **Examples** :-

❖ "In project management, you don't tie a bundle of wood with one hand. It's important to allocate adequate resources and manpower to ensure successful project completion."

❖ "When launching a new product, you don't tie a bundle of wood with one hand. It's crucial to involve multiple teams and departments to handle various aspects like production, marketing, and customer support effectively."

"Paint the town red"-

> **Meaning:** - to go out and enjoy yourself by drinking alcohol, dancing, laughing with friends, etc.:

> **Examples: -**

❖ "I'm ready to paint the town red with a few of my closest friends"

❖ "After successfully completing the project, the team decided to paint the town red by going out for a celebratory dinner."

"A pot of gold"-

> **Meaning** :- A positive outcome or valuable result obtained through effective teamwork.

> **Examples** :-

❖ "Our seamless collaboration left us with a pot of gold—a highly successful project that exceeded all expectations."

❖ "The team's collective efforts and shared expertise left us with a pot of gold—a groundbreaking innovation that revolutionised our industry."

"Quarrelsome sheep"-

> **Meaning** :- A person who tends to create conflict or problems within a group

> **Examples** :-

❖ "The new employee was a bit of a quarrelsome sheep, always causing tension in the team"

❖ "In a corporate meeting, the presence of quarrelsome sheep among the team led to constant arguments and hindered progress on the project."

"To get on like a house on fire"-

> **Meaning** :- Describing a strong and positive working relationship between individuals or teams

> **Examples:-**

❖ "Since we started working together, we've been getting on like a house on fire and have accomplished a lot."

❖ "The marketing and sales departments get on like a house on fire, constantly supporting each other to achieve their targets."

"To have someone's back"-

> **Meaning** :- Support and assistance in achieving common goals.

> **Examples :-**

* ❖ "I have got your back, so let's collaborate and deliver the project on time."

* ❖ "Even in challenging situations, I have got your back, and we will overcome any obstacles together."

"Cannot sleepwalk into technical debt"-

> **Meaning :-** The risk of accumulating technical debt due to poor technical decisions

> **Examples :-**

* ❖ "We need to be proactive and cannot sleepwalk into technical debt."

* ❖ "When implementing new software, we must carefully evaluate potential risks and avoid rushing into decisions, as we cannot sleepwalk into technical debt."

"Learning the ropes"-

> **Meaning:-** Still gaining experience and knowledge on cloud computing

> **Examples :-**

* ❖ "Our team is still learning the ropes on cloud, but we are making progress."

* ❖ "In our transition to cloud computing, we are still learning the ropes on the cloud to effectively manage data storage and accessibility."

"Stream the email on Skype"-

> **Meaning** :- Use of technology to communicate a message

> **Examples** :-

❖ "I will stream the email on Skype so everyone can join the discussion remotely."

❖ "To ensure everyone is on the same page, I will stream the email on Skype and go through its contents with the remote team members."

"Stormy Relationship"-

> **Meaning** :- A state of conflict or strained interaction between two or more parties.

> **Examples** :-

❖ "The stormy relationship between the project manager and the team lead created constant tension and hindered effective collaboration."

❖ "The stormy relationship between the two departments resulted in frequent disagreements and a lack of cooperation, impacting overall productivity."

"My Hackles Are Up"-

> **Meaning** :- Feeling defensive or on guard.

> Examples :-

  ❖ "During a team meeting, when a colleague makes an accusatory comment, you might say, My hackles are up because I feel personally attacked."

  ❖ "During a team meeting, when a colleague makes an accusatory comment, you might say, My hackles are up because I feel personally attacked."

"Let the poor wretch go"-

> **Meaning** :- To release an underperforming or unsuitable employee from their position.

> **Examples :-**

  ❖ "After careful evaluation, the management decided to let the poor wretch go due to consistently poor performance."

  ❖ "The team leader reluctantly made the difficult call to let the poor wretch go after numerous warnings and failed improvement attempts."

"Limited Runway"-

> **Meaning** :- Limited time or deadline

> **Examples :-**

  ❖ "We need to make sure we finish the project within the limited runway provided"

- ❖ "Due to the limited runway, the team had to prioritise essential features and cut back on non-essential ones to meet the project deadline."

"Hang One's Hat And Wait"-

- ➢ **Meaning** :- Avoiding delays caused by slow response or action from others

- ➢ **Examples :-**

  - ❖ "We can't hang our hat and wait for them to finish their part, we need to find a way to keep the project moving."

  - ❖ "Our team emphasises efficient time management, so we avoid hanging our hats and waiting for others who are slow in completing their assigned tasks."

CHAPTER 7

Project Management

"Prune The Bushes"-

> **Meaning** :- To remove unnecessary or irrelevant elements to reach a clear and effective decision.

> **Examples :-**

❖ "In a meeting, we need to prune the bushes and focus on the essential points to make a timely decision."

❖ "When analysing a project proposal, it's important to prune the bushes and eliminate unnecessary details to evaluate its viability efficiently."

"Relentless Pursuit Of Creativity"-

> **Meaning** :- An unwavering commitment to innovation, creativity and originality in the production of goods or services.

> **Examples :-**

- ❖ "Our company prides itself on its relentless pursuit of creativity in its marketing campaigns, always looking for new and innovative ways to reach our target audience."

- ❖ "The team's success is attributed to their shared value of a relentless pursuit of creativity, which fosters a culture of continuous improvement and novel solutions."

"To Model Out The Costs"-

> **Meaning :-** Consider the potential costs in detail before making a decision or taking action.

> **Examples :-**

- ❖ "In financial planning, if you model out those costs, you can determine the feasibility of an investment and its potential returns."

- ❖ "When assessing project risks, if you model out those costs, you can identify potential financial implications and allocate resources accordingly."

"Cutting Very Close"-

> **Meaning :-** To be very close to a deadline or finishing a task just in time

> Examples :-

  - ❖ "We finished the project just in time. It was cutting very close."

  - ❖ "Our project was cutting very close to the deadline, requiring us to work late nights to ensure everything was finished on time."

"Moving Parts"-

> Meaning :- The situation or task at hand is complex and involves multiple interconnected elements.

> Examples :-

  - ❖ "During the project review, the team leader summarised the situation by saying, "So that's a very quick spill, there are a lot of moving parts there.""

  - ❖ "In the boardroom, the CEO acknowledged the intricate nature of the upcoming merger, stating, "So that's a very quick spill, there are a lot of moving parts there.""

"Change Freeze Boundaries"-

> Meaning :- Setting limits on changes that can be made to a particular system or process

> Examples :-

  - ❖ "The company set change freeze boundaries on the HR system during the critical period of hiring"

❖ "The IT department set change freeze boundaries during the software development cycle to avoid any last-minute changes."

"Continue In The New Construct"-

> **Meaning :-** To express commitment to continue in a new situation or environment

> **Examples :-**

❖ "We will continue to support the project despite the shift in management and the new construct."

❖ "As we enter the new fiscal year, we will continue to deliver high-quality services in the new construct."

"Clearly Delineated"-

> **Meaning :-** Something that is clearly defined or outlined

> **Examples :-**

❖ "We need to have a clearly delineated plan of action to achieve our goals."

❖ "A clearly delineated dress code policy ensures that employees maintain a professional appearance in the workplace."

"Far-Reaching Impact"-

> **Meaning:** -The significant and long-lasting consequences resulting from a particular decision or action.

> **Examples :-**

❖ "The CEO's decision to restructure the company had a far-reaching impact on employee morale and productivity."

❖ "The implementation of new technology had a far-reaching impact on the company's operational efficiency and cost savings."

"To Make Good On One's Promises"-

> **Meaning** :-The ability to fulfill commitments and deliver on promises.

> **Examples :-**

❖ "In a corporate project, I will be able to make good on my promises by meeting all the deadlines and delivering high-quality work within the agreed-upon scope."

❖ "As a team leader, I will be able to make good on my promises by effectively communicating with team members, providing necessary resources, and ensuring that everyone meets their individual goals to achieve the desired outcome."

"Make It To The Plate"-

> **Meaning :-** Taking responsibility for completing a task or achieving a goal.

> **Examples :-**

❖ "John, make it to the plate this time and submit the report before the deadline."

❖ "We need to make it to the plate this time and deliver the project on schedule to maintain client satisfaction."

"Deliverables Kicking Goals"-

> **Meaning** :- The deliverables were highly successful and exceeded expectations.

> **Examples :-**

❖ "Despite the tight deadline, the team's deliverables were kicking goals, impressing the client with exceptional quality."

❖ "The marketing campaign's deliverables were kicking goals, resulting in a significant increase in customer engagement and sales."

"To Flex One's Muscles "-

> **Meaning :-** Demonstrating strength, power, or capability in a given situation.

> **Examples :-**

❖ "During a negotiation, John flexed his muscles by presenting a well-researched and compelling argument, showcasing his expertise and influence."

❖ "The team leader flexed their muscles by delegating tasks effectively and motivating team members, resulting in improved productivity and successful project completion."

"Shift Left"-

➤ **Meaning** :- Moving the person, process, or technology closer to the customer, resulting in a faster and more efficient and effective resolution

➤ **Examples :-**

❖ "By incorporating customer feedback early in the product design phase, we can "shift left" and avoid costly redesigns and iterations later on."

❖ "By encouraging open and transparent communication within teams, we can "shift left" and address any conflicts or misunderstandings before they escalate into bigger issues."

"No Rhyme Or Reason"-

➤ **Meaning:-** To be without any obvious reasonable explanation/If something happens or is done without rhyme or reason, there seems to be no logical reason for it to happen or be done.

> **Examples :-**

❖ "He picked people on a whim, without rhyme or reason."

❖ "The company's budget cuts had no rhyme or reason; valuable departments were affected while unnecessary expenses remained untouched."

CHAPTER 8

Risk Management

"To Smell Panic"-

> **Meaning :-** Detecting a state of anxiety or unease indicating a critical situation.

> **Examples :-**

- ❖ "During a major system failure, the CEO entered the control room and said, I smell panic. Stay calm and focus on finding a solution."

- ❖ "In a high-pressure deadline situation, the project manager walked into the team's workspace and declared, I smell panic. Let's regroup, prioritise tasks, and work together to meet the deadline."

"To Run For Cover"-

> **Meaning** :- Taking action to protect oneself or one's company from a competitive threat

> **Examples** :-

  ❖ "The company is running for cover in response to the new competitor entering the market."

  ❖ "During the company's financial crisis, the CEO was seen running for cover by laying off employees to cut costs."

"To Smell Blood In The Water"-

> **Meaning** :- Sensing an opportunity to exploit a weakness or vulnerability in a competitive situation.

> **Examples** :-

  ❖ "During a product launch, rival companies are already smelling blood in the water, eager to capitalise on any missteps."

  ❖ "In a corporate reorganisation, employees are on edge as rumours circulate, and some individuals are already smelling blood in the water, hoping to secure promotions or take advantage of the situation."

"Your Career Is Already Hanging By A Thread"-

> **Meaning** :- Your professional success is in imminent danger or on the verge of collapse.

➤ **Examples :-**

❖ "Your constant missed deadlines and lack of accountability have put you in a situation where your career is already hanging by a thread."

❖ "The major client's dissatisfaction with your performance and the series of costly mistakes you made have left your career hanging by a thread."

"Turbulent Times"-

➤ **Meaning:-** Difficult and unpredictable circumstances or events.

➤ Examples :-

❖ "During turbulent times, companies face economic instability, market fluctuations, and increased competition, requiring adaptability and resilience to navigate the challenges successfully."

❖ "The company's leadership team demonstrated strong decision-making and effective crisis management strategies to steer the organisation through turbulent times caused by a global pandemic, ensuring business continuity and employee well-being."

"Fight Chaos With Chaos"-

> **Meaning** :- Embrace the unpredictable nature of a situation and respond with flexibility and creativity.

> **Examples** :-

❖ "In a rapidly changing market, companies fight chaos with chaos by continuously innovating and adapting their strategies to stay ahead."

❖ "During a project with unforeseen challenges, the team fights chaos with chaos by quickly adjusting their plans and finding alternative solutions to meet the deadline."

"Cut Corners"-

> **Meaning** :- Taking shortcuts or skipping necessary steps in order to save time or meet deadlines.

> **Examples** :-

❖ "Due to the project's tight deadline, they decided to cut corners and skip the final quality check."

❖ "In an attempt to finish the report quickly, she cut corners by omitting important data analysis, resulting in an incomplete and inaccurate document."

"To Be Slammed At Work"-

> **Meaning** :- To have a lot of work to do.

> **Examples** :-

  ❖ "I am so slammed next week, I have back-to-back meetings and multiple project deadlines to meet."

  ❖ "I am so slammed next week, I won't have much time for anything else as I need to focus on completing urgent tasks."

"Take Some Minutes Back"-

> **Meaning** :- Ending a discussion or meeting early to allocate additional time for other tasks or breaks.

> **Examples** :-

  ❖ "Alright guys we will close it there and take 25 minutes back. Let's use this time to prepare for the upcoming presentation."

  ❖ "Alright guys we will close it there and take 25 minutes back. Use this time to catch up on emails or take a short break before the next meeting."

"I Think We Are Up To Time Guys"-

> **Meaning** :- Allotted time for a particular task or meeting is almost over.

> **Examples :-**

  ❖ "During a team meeting, the project manager says, I think we are up to time, guys. Let's wrap up the discussion and finalise the action plan."

  ❖ "In a boardroom presentation, a presenter realises, I think we are up to time, guys. We need to quickly cover the remaining slides and leave room for questions."

"A Lot Of Ground To Cover"-

> **Meaning :-** Having a significant amount of work or tasks to complete within a limited time frame.

> **Examples :-**

  ❖ "We need to cover a lot of ground in American History before the exam date."

  ❖ "The project deadline is approaching fast, and we have a lot of ground to cover in three days, so we must avoid any time-wasting activities and stay focused on our objectives."

"Get One's Bearings On Something"-

> **Meaning :-** To familiarise oneself with or understand something.

> **Examples :-**

  ❖ "I need to get my bearings on the new project, can you give me this weekend to complete the task?"

❖ "We're implementing a new software system, give me this weekend to get my bearings on that."

"To Do A Rush Job"-

➤ **Meaning** :- Having to complete a task quickly due to limited time.

➤ **Examples** :-

❖ "I had to do a rush job on the presentation because the client moved up the deadline."

❖ "I had to do a rush job on the report as my colleague fell ill and I had to cover their workload."

"Defining Renaissance"-

➤ **Meaning** :- The process of bringing about significant and positive change in a particular area.

➤ **Examples** :-

❖ "Defining Renaissance in the workplace involves transforming outdated systems and processes to improve efficiency and productivity."

❖ "Implementing new technologies and adopting innovative strategies is crucial for the Defining Renaissance of a company in the digital age."

"Open, Transparent, And Obvious Process"-

> **Meaning** :- A process that is clear, visible, and easily understood by all involved parties.

> **Examples** :-

  ❖ "When making strategic decisions, it is crucial to follow an open, transparent, and obvious process to ensure that everyone's input is considered and that the final choice is clear to everyone involved."

  ❖ "In negotiations, an open, transparent, and obvious process helps build trust between parties and ensures that all information and terms are clearly communicated, leading to fair and mutually beneficial agreements."

"To Hide A Sheep"-

> **Meaning** :- Evaluating the presence of hidden flaws or agenda in a given context.

> **Examples** :-

  ❖ "During a team meeting, a manager asks, Are you hiding any sheep in this presentation? to gauge if someone is concealing critical information that could impact the team's progress."

  ❖ "In a negotiation, a participant asks, Are you hiding any sheep in this presentation? to question the other party's transparency and sincerity in their proposed terms."

"To Be On A Thin Ice"-

> **Meaning :-** The situation is delicate and there is a significant lack of trust within the alliance.

> **Examples :-**

❖ "Due to a series of breaches in confidentiality, the alliance is on very thin ice."

❖ "The alliance's failure to meet critical deadlines has put their relationship on very thin ice."

"To Burn Bridges"-

> **Meaning :-** To severe relationships and damage trust.

> **Examples :-**

❖ ": In my previous job, I made sure to maintain positive relationships with colleagues, so I didn't just burn bridges behind me when I left for a new opportunity."

❖ "When transitioning to a new team, I took the time to communicate effectively and resolve any conflicts, ensuring I didn't just burn bridges behind me and maintained strong professional connections."

"To Lie Through Your Teeth"-

> **Meaning :-** Everyone is dishonest and untruthful.

> Examples :-

  ❖ "During a team meeting, the project manager caught a group of employees providing false updates, saying, "All of you are lying through your teeth about the project's progress."

  ❖ "In a negotiation, a client accused the sales team of providing misleading information, stating, "All of you are lying through your teeth to secure the deal.""

"Your Guess Is As Good As Mine"-

> **Meaning :-** I have no more information than you do

> **Examples :-**

  ❖ "When asked about the potential impact of the new policy, the manager replied, Your guess is as good as mine."

  ❖ "When it comes to which project we should prioritise next, your guess is as good as mine."

"To Scare People On The Outset"-

> **Meaning** :- People feeling fearful or apprehensive at the beginning of a new project or endeavour due to lack of clarity or predictability.

> **Examples :-**

  ❖ "The sudden reorganisation of the company scared people on the outset, as they were unsure about their roles and responsibilities."

❖ "The announcement of potential layoffs
scared people on the outset, creating a sense
of insecurity and anxiety among employees."

"To Not Be Out Of The Woods"-

➤ **Meaning** :- The current situation is still
challenging and unpredictable.

➤ **Examples** :-

❖ "We are not out of the woods yet in terms of
financial stability, so we need to continue
making budget cuts and reducing expenses."

❖ "Although we have made progress, we are not
out of the woods yet with the project deadline.
We need to stay focused and work diligently
to meet the target."

"To Look A Little Thrown"-

➤ **Meaning** :- To appear slightly overwhelmed or
surprised by a sudden difficulty or change in
circumstances.

➤ **Examples** :-

❖ "During a meeting, a team member receives
surprising feedback. Their manager notices
their reaction and says, You look thrown.
Let's discuss it further to address any
concerns."

❖ "In a presentation, an unexpected technical
glitch occurs. The audience notices the
speaker's momentary confusion and whispers,

They look thrown. They'll quickly recover and continue."

"To Dump Something On One's Lap"-

> **Meaning** :- To burden someone with an unexpected task or problem.

> **Examples** :-

❖ "I am sorry to dump this in your lap, but the client just requested urgent changes to the project."

❖ "I am sorry to dump this in your lap, but the server crashed, and we need you to troubleshoot it immediately."

"Swift Left"-

> **Meaning** :- To act quickly and decisively

> **Examples** :-

❖ "We need to take a swift left and address the issue before it gets worse."

❖ "In the brainstorming session, when a new idea is proposed, the team leader encourages everyone to take a swift left and start implementing it without delay."

"Intrinsically Important"-

> **Meaning** :- Recognizing and acknowledging the inherent significance or worth of something.

> Examples :-

* ❖ "In a corporate work environment, it is intrinsically important to recognize and appreciate the individual contributions of employees to foster a positive and motivated team."

* ❖ "When making strategic decisions, considering the long-term impact on company values and ethics is intrinsically important to maintain a reputable and sustainable business."

"Authenticity Over Cosmetic Harmony"-

> **Meaning** :- Prioritising genuine and real over superficial or appearance-focused

> **Examples** :-

* ❖ "The company values authenticity over cosmetic harmony and focuses on meaningful, impactful work."

* ❖ "In the boardroom, the CEO emphasised authenticity over cosmetic harmony by encouraging open and honest discussions, even if they led to conflicts."

"Aesthetic, The General Appeal Of Something."-

> **Meaning** :- concerned with beauty or the appreciation of beauty.

> **Examples :-**

  ❖ "the pictures give great aesthetic pleasure"

  ❖ "During the meeting, the executives considered the aesthetic of the office space before finalising the renovation plans."

"Remain Switched On"-

> **Meaning :-** Stay alert and focused

> **Examples :-**

  ❖ "We have to remain switched on during this critical time in the project to avoid mistakes and meet our deadlines."

  ❖ "In a high-pressure project, it's important to remain switched on to quickly identify and address the most critical tasks."

"Knuckle Down"-

> **Meaning :-** Focusing and working hard on a task or project

> **Examples :-**

  ❖ "We need to knuckle down and finish this project by the end of the week."

  ❖ "Let's knuckle down and prioritise our tasks to ensure we meet our targets for the quarter."

"Reflective Supervision"-

> **Meaning :-** A form of supervision that focuses on reflection and self-awareness

> **Examples :-**

❖ "The new manager implemented a reflective supervision program to help employees develop self-awareness and improve their performance."

❖ "Reflective supervision sessions provide an opportunity for managers to offer guidance and support to their team members, leading to improved performance and job satisfaction."

"Always Chasing Our Tails"-

> **Meaning** :- Continuously being busy without making progress

> **Examples :-**

❖ "We need to be more organised; otherwise, we'll always be chasing our tails."

❖ "We're always chasing our tails because we underestimate the time required for each task."

"Roll Up One's Sleeves Attitude"-

> **Meaning :-** to prepare for hard work

> **Examples :-**

❖ " There's a lot of work to do, so roll up your sleeves and get busy."

❖ "Before the major product launch, the team adopted a roll-up-your-sleeves attitude by conducting thorough market research and refining the marketing strategy."

"To Cover Up For Someone"-

> **Meaning** :- Taking responsibility for someone else's mistake

> **Examples** :-

❖ "I'll cover up for you, but don't let it happen again."

❖ "In a project meeting, if a team member makes a mistake, I will cover up for them by taking the blame and explaining it as a collective oversight."

"Blur Work-Life Balance"-

> **Meaning** :- The boundaries between work and personal life becoming unclear

> **Examples** :-

❖ "Many employees are complaining about the blurring of work-life balance since they started working from home."

❖ "Working late nights and weekends regularly, neglecting personal commitments and hobbies, resulting in a blurring of work-life balance."

"Maintain The Operating Rhythm"-

> **Meaning** :- Sustaining an efficient and effective operational flow.

> **Examples** :-

❖ "During a project, it is essential to maintain the operating rhythm by regularly reviewing progress and addressing any bottlenecks to ensure smooth workflow optimization."

❖ "In a corporate setting, maintaining the operating rhythm involves adhering to established processes and timelines, enabling teams to work cohesively towards their objectives and deliver results efficiently."

"To Work Someone To The Bones"-

> **Meaning** :- To work someone excessively or until they are exhausted

> **Examples** :-

❖ "He complained to his colleague that Linda works him to the bones with all her demands"

❖ "Linda works me to the bones, constantly assigning additional tasks and expecting them to be completed within unrealistic deadlines."

"To Use One's Claws"-

> **Meaning** :- Being slightly more assertive in a professional setting.

> **Examples :-**

  ❖ "During negotiations, I might have used my claws a little to secure a better deal."

  ❖ "In a team meeting, I might have used my claws a little to make my point more effectively."

"I Like To Keep It A Bit Light."-

> **Meaning :-** Keep it light means...don't be pushy, don't get over emotional, keep it light, take it easy, are all right.

> **Examples :-**

  ❖ "During team meetings, I like to keep it a bit light to encourage open discussion and creativity."

  ❖ "Even in high-pressure situations, I believe in keeping it a bit light to reduce stress and promote a positive work environment."

"He Has A Checkered Past"-

> **Meaning :-** a past history of having done bad things or been in trouble

> **Examples :-**

  ❖ "The senator has a checkered past."

  ❖ "Although he has a checkered past, he has shown significant improvement in his work ethic."

"Gossip Mongering"-

> **Meaning** :-Engaging in spreading rumours or idle talk about colleagues or work-related matters.

> **Examples** :-

❖ "Gossip mongering can create a toxic work environment and hinder productivity."

❖ "Engaging in gossip mongering can damage professional relationships and erode trust among team members."

"How Have You Been Holding Up?"-

> **Meaning** :- A question asked to inquire about the well-being of a colleague or employee

> **Examples** :-

❖ "In a performance review, a manager begins the conversation by saying, "I wanted to check in on how you've been holding up lately. Are there any work-related stressors we should address?"

❖ "During a team meeting, the team leader asks, "How have you been holding up? Any challenges or concerns affecting your well-being?""

"Shit-Storm"-

> **Meaning** :- A chaotic or problematic situation

> **Examples :-**

  ❖ "After the merger, there was a shit-storm of layoffs and reorganisation"

  ❖ "The miscommunication between the teams caused a shit-storm, leading to delays in the project and budget overruns."

"Artificial Hoohah"-

> **Meaning :-** Superficial or unnecessary activities that create distractions and hinder productivity in the corporate work environment.

> **Examples :-**

  ❖ "The team wasted valuable time discussing artificial hoohah instead of focusing on the project deadline."

  ❖ "Management decided to eliminate all artificial hoohah during meetings to improve efficiency and keep discussions relevant."

"Everything Gone Out Of The Window"-

> **Meaning:-** Disregarded or disregarding important principles or norms in the corporate work environment.

> **Examples :-**

  ❖ "Recently, professionalism and teamwork have all gone out of the window in our office, leading to conflicts and decreased productivity."

* "The company's focus on employee well-being has recently gone out of the window, resulting in increased stress and burnout among the staff."

"Cynicism Disguised As Benevolence"-

> **Meaning** :- Someone feigns kindness and goodwill but actually holds cynical or selfish intentions.

> **Examples :-**

* "In a team meeting, a colleague offers to take on a task, claiming it's to help others, but secretly hopes to gain favoritism from the boss."

* "A supervisor presents a new policy as a measure to enhance employee well-being, but it's actually a cost-cutting measure disguised as benevolence."

"To Sneak Up On Someone"-

> **Meaning :-** To approach someone or something in a sneaky, furtive manner so as not to be noticed.

> **Examples :-**

* "We don't want the guards to see us, so we'll need to sneak up from the back."

* "During a meeting, a colleague approaches from behind and startles you. You say, You

don't sneak up on me like that to remind them to announce their presence next time."

"There's Nothing Kinkier And More Taboo Than"-

> **Meaning** :- Engaging in rumours and personal discussions about colleagues or superiors.

> **Examples :-**

❖ "There's nothing kinkier and more taboo than spreading workplace gossip about your boss's personal life."

❖ "There's nothing kinkier and more taboo than indulging in office gossip about a coworker's promotion."

"To Give A Delighted Whoop"-

> **Meaning :-** Expressed joy or excitement in a loud, energetic way

> **Examples :-**

❖ "When I told him we landed the big account, he gave me a delighted whoop."

❖ "When the team achieved the sales target, their manager's announcement gave them a delighted whoop."

"To Not Get Under One's Skin"-

> **Meaning** :- To not irritate or provoke in any way.

> **Examples :-**

> ❖ "During a team meeting, one colleague repeatedly interrupts others and undermines their ideas. Frustrated, the team leader sternly reminds them, Don't get under my skin."

> ❖ "In a negotiation between two companies, one party starts making personal attacks instead of focusing on the business aspects. The other party firmly states, Let's keep it professional and constructive. " Don't get under my skin."

"Sob story"-

> **Meaning :-** A tale of personal difficulties or struggles aimed at evoking sympathy.

> **Examples :-**

> ❖ "Don't tell your sob story to me; just get the job done."

> ❖ "Don't tell your sob story to me; take responsibility for your mistakes."

"Jousting Accident."-

> **Meaning :-** An unfortunate incident or mistake that occurs within the corporate work environment.

> **Examples :-**

> ❖ "During a heated debate, two colleagues engaged in a jousting accident by exchanging sharp and hurtful remarks."

- ❖ "The email thread turned into a jousting accident as team members argued passionately without considering the impact on their working relationships."

"Conspiracy theorist"-

- ➢ **Meaning** :- A person who believes in and promotes alternative explanations or hidden agendas behind events or situations.

- ➢ **Examples** :-

    - ❖ "During the team meeting, John, a conspiracy theorist, raised doubts about the company's financial reports, suggesting there might be undisclosed discrepancies."

    - ❖ "Sarah's reputation as a conspiracy theorist affects her professional relationships, as colleagues hesitate to collaborate with her due to her unfounded claims about office politics."

"Falling Off The Horse"-

- ➢ **Meaning** :- Failing to perform up to expectations

- ➢ **Examples** :-

    - ❖ "It's important to identify the reasons why employees are falling off the horse and work with them to improve their performance."

    - ❖ "Sarah forgot to follow the proper meeting etiquette, falling off the horse in front of her colleagues."

"Short Fuse Individual"-

> **Meaning** :- The person is easily angered or loses their temper quickly.

> **Examples** :-

  ❖ "During a team meeting, he has a short fuse and often reacts angrily to criticism or suggestions."

  ❖ "In the corporate work environment, his short fuse creates a tense atmosphere, affecting team dynamics and productivity."

"Volley Of Paragraphs"-

> **Meaning** :- A large number of paragraphs or sections of text

> **Examples** :-

  ❖ "The report was filled with a volley of paragraphs, making it difficult to read."

  ❖ "During the email exchange, there was a volley of paragraphs discussing the project's requirements."

CHAPTER 9

Work Ethics and Culture

"To Feed Dirty Laundry"-

> **Meaning:** - you disapprove of their discussing or arguing about unpleasant or private things in front of other people. (Leaking our weakness)/to say very embarrassing things in front of other people

> **Examples:** -

❖ "I hate going to family reunions because my uncle always airs his dirty laundry and we all feel embarrassed for my aunt."

❖ "During the team meeting, John and Lisa aired their dirty laundry, arguing about their conflicting work styles."

"To Be Good Corporate Citizens"-

> **Meaning:** - Encouraging ethical and socially responsible behaviour in business practices

> **Examples:** -

❖ "As a company, we need to prioritise being good corporate citizens and give back to society."

❖ "Let's be good corporate citizens by keeping our colleagues informed about important updates and changes."

"To Take Time Without A Dime"-

> **Meaning :-** Someone has wasted your time

> **Examples :-**

❖ "That meeting was a complete waste of time. You took my time without a dime."

❖ "During the meeting, you kept discussing irrelevant topics, and it felt like you took my time without a dime."

"Play One For A Fool"-

> **Meaning :-** To deceive or trick someone for one's own benefit

> **Examples :-**

❖ "I knew he was lying, so I played him for a fool and got what I wanted."

❖ "A manager tricked a subordinate into taking on an extra workload without any valid reason, just played him for a fool."

"Big Fat Liar"-

➢ **Meaning** :- Someone who constantly tells significant lies.

➢ **Examples :-**

❖ "John claimed that he had completed his assigned tasks, but his colleagues quickly realised he was a big fat liar when they discovered he hadn't even started working on them."

❖ "During a job interview, the hiring manager discovered that the candidate was a big fat liar when his claimed achievements turned out to be completely fabricated."

"To Burn A Lot Of Bridges"-

➢ **Meaning :-** You will damage many relationships and create conflicts due to poor communication skills.

➢ **Examples :-**

❖ "By consistently ignoring emails and not responding promptly, you are gonna burn a lot of bridges with your colleagues."

❖ "If you speak disrespectfully to your superiors and peers, you are gonna burn a lot of bridges and hinder your professional growth."

"To freeze someone out"-

- ➤ **Meaning** :- Experience a prolonged lack of communication or exclusion from someone.

- ➤ **Examples** :-

  - ❖ "Despite my efforts to reach out, she is still freezing me out, and I'm left in the dark about important project updates."

  - ❖ "In team meetings, she intentionally avoids including me in discussions and decision-making, freezing me out from the collaborative process."

"This Is The Nature Of The Beast"-

- ➤ **Meaning** :- Inherent characteristics or inherent challenges that arise in a given situation.

- ➤ **Examples** :-

  - ❖ "Dealing with diverse stakeholder opinions and conflicting priorities is challenging, but this is the nature of the beast in project management."

  - ❖ "Meeting tight deadlines while ensuring quality work can be demanding, but this is the nature of the beast in a fast-paced corporate environment."

"That's illegal in twenty different ways" -

> **Meaning** :- Referring to a violation or non-compliance with rules, regulations, or policies in multiple ways.

> **Examples :-**

❖ "During the meeting, John disclosed confidential company information to a competitor, which is illegal in twenty different ways."

❖ "The team decided to manipulate financial records to hide losses, but that's illegal in twenty different ways and can lead to severe legal consequences."

"Shadow Environment" -

> **Meaning**: - A secure and protected workspace

> **Examples: -**

❖ "We need to ensure the project is done in a shadow environment."

❖ "The company implemented a shadow environment for performance evaluation, allowing supervisors to observe employees' day-to-day activities without their knowledge."

"Falling Out"-

> **Meaning:** - A disagreement or dispute with someone, leading to a breakdown in the relationship

> **Examples:** -

❖ "They fell out over a disagreement on the project's direction."

❖ "The falling out between the two executives led to a breakdown in communication and collaboration, affecting the entire team's productivity."

"Don't Get Mad, Get Even"-

> **Meaning:** - to become angry

> **Examples:** -

❖ "When a colleague takes credit for your work, don't get mad, get even by addressing the issue with your supervisor and providing evidence of your contributions."

❖ "If a competitor uses unethical tactics, don't get mad, get even by focusing on improving your own strategies and delivering superior products or services."

"To Knock Someone Out Cold"-

> **Meaning:** - To completely overpower or defeat someone in a confrontational situation.

> **Examples: -**

❖ "During a heated debate in a team meeting, your testimony knocks him out cold by presenting irrefutable evidence that supports your proposal."

❖ "In a workplace investigation, your testimony knocks him out cold as you provide compelling accounts and facts that discredit his version of events."

"Can't Put Cork Back In The Bottle"-

> **Meaning** :- Once something is done or said, it cannot be undone

> **Examples** :-

❖ "Once the data breach occurred, it was impossible to put the cork back in the bottle."

❖ "The company's unethical practices were exposed, and they couldn't put the cork back in the bottle, resulting in a significant loss of customer trust."

"Strong-Arm Someone"-

> **Meaning** :-Using force or pressure to make someone do something against their will.

> **Examples** :-

❖ "In a corporate setting, the manager strong-armed the employee to work overtime by threatening their job security."

❖ "The project team was strong-armed into accepting unrealistic deadlines by the upper management, leaving them with no choice but to comply."

"More The Merrier"-

➢ **Meaning:** The greater the number of participants, the more enjoyable and productive outcome.

➢ **Examples:-**

❖ "Can I bring my friends to the party? Of course, the more the merrier!"

❖ "Let's invite all team members to the brainstorming session. More the merrier, as it will bring diverse perspectives."

"To Storm Out"-

➢ **Meaning** :- To express anger or frustration in an aggressive manner

➢ **Examples :-**

❖ "I don't understand why you had to storm out like that. We could have talked it out like adults."

❖ "A colleague abruptly leaves the meeting in anger, leaving others confused, and someone asks, Why did you storm out like that? Come out like that."

"Effed Up Language"-

> **Meaning:** - The quality and effectiveness of verbal or written communication are severely flawed.

> **Examples** :-

  ❖ "During the team meeting, John's language was seriously effed up as he used offensive and inappropriate words while presenting his ideas."

  ❖ "The email sent by the employee to the client had grammatical errors, unclear explanations, and inappropriate language, indicating that their language was seriously effed up."

"To Skimp On Linens"-

> **Meaning** :- Emphasising the importance of paying close attention to details and not neglecting any aspect.

> **Examples** :-

  ❖ "We've got plenty of cheese so don't skimp on it."

  ❖ "In a presentation, don't skimp on linens; make sure your slides are polished and visually appealing, paying attention to formatting and design."

"Tad Eccentric Individual"-

> **Meaning :-** a person with an unusual or odd personality.

> **Examples :-**

❖ "Her eccentricity in problem-solving led her to discover creative solutions that others had overlooked."

❖ "While her work output was exceptional, her eccentricity sometimes made her interactions with clients a tad awkward."

"To Be Sick And Tired Of One's Antics"-

> **Meaning :-** Frustration and annoyance with the inappropriate or disruptive actions of an individual in the workplace.

> **Examples :-**

❖ "During team meetings, I am sick and tired of your antics of constantly interrupting and derailing the discussion."

❖ "I am sick and tired of your antics of spreading rumours and gossiping, which creates a negative work environment."

"To Snitch On Someone"-

> **Meaning :-**Reporting or disclosing someone's wrongdoing or confidential information to a superior or authority.

➢ **Examples :-**

❖ "He was the one snitching on me, jeopardising our team's project by leaking sensitive data to a competitor."

❖ "During the meeting, I discovered that he was the one snitching on me, undermining trust within the team and hindering collaboration."

"Stick A Knife To The Heart And Apple In The Mouth"-

➢ **Meaning :-** A phrase used to describe a deeply hurtful or treacherous action

➢ **Examples :-**

❖ "Finding out that my trusted colleague had been stealing from the company was like someone sticking a knife to my heart and putting an apple in my mouth."

❖ "The CEO's decisive action of sticking a knife to the heart and apple in the mouth involved promptly addressing the security breach and implementing stringent measures to prevent any further data breaches."

"To Be Wired With A Stereotype"-

➢ **Meaning :-** Having a preconceived notion about a person or group based on their characteristics

> **Examples :-**

  ❖ "We tend to stereotype people based on their age, gender, or ethnicity, which can lead to discrimination."

  ❖ "During brainstorming sessions, we often overlook valuable contributions from non-technical team members because we are wired with a stereotype."

"To Step On One's Toes"-

> **Meaning :-** Hurt or offend someone.

> **Examples :-**

  ❖ "I don't want to step on your toes, so please let me know if my involvement in this project is causing any issues."

  ❖ "I don't want to step on your toes, but I have a suggestion that might improve our teamwork."

"Penny-Pinching"-

> **Meaning :-** Practising frugality or extreme cost-saving measures.

> **Examples :-**

  ❖ "The company implemented penny-pinching strategies to reduce expenses and increase profitability, such as reducing travel expenses and switching to cost-effective suppliers."

❖ ": The department was under pressure to cut costs, leading to penny-pinching measures like reducing office supplies and minimising unnecessary expenses."

"They Are Quite Roomy"-

➢ **Meaning** :- There is ample space or opportunity for various aspects within a given situation.

➢ **Examples :-**

❖ "In terms of meeting rooms, they are quite roomy, allowing for comfortable seating and effective collaboration among team members."

❖ "The company's budget for innovation projects is quite roomy, enabling the exploration of new ideas and technologies."

"Mangled Kittens In The Hot Sun"-

➢ **Meaning** :-Dealing with a severe and urgent problem or disaster.

➢ **Examples :-**

❖ "The CEO had to handle mangled kittens in the hot sun when a major security breach occurred in the company's database."

❖ "The team had to engage in mangled kittens in the hot sun when a crucial client threatened to terminate their contract due to a serious quality issue."

"To Be The Fall Guy."-

> ➢ **Meaning:** Taking the blame or responsibility for a situation or outcome, often undeservedly.

> ➢ **Examples :-**

> ❖ "During the meeting, when the project failed to meet its deadline, John stepped up and said, I am the fall guy. It was my oversight."

> ❖ "When the company's financial results were disappointing, the CEO took the lead and stated, I am the fall guy. I should have made better decisions."

"To Not Be On The Hook"-

> ➢ **Meaning :-** Expressing a strong desire to avoid being held responsible or liable for a particular matter.

> ➢ **Examples :-**

> ❖ "I don't want to be on the hook for it. It's not my responsibility."

> ❖ "I certainly don't want to be on the hook for it. Let someone else handle the consequences."

"Keep One Honest"-

> ➢ **Meaning :-** Ensuring transparency and integrity in actions and decisions.

> **Examples :-**

- ❖ "Having a weekly catch-up with my manager keeps me honest and ensures we are on the same page."

- ❖ "During project reviews, asking probing questions helps keep one honest about the progress and challenges faced."

"Cutting Off The Nose To Spite The Face"-

> **Meaning** :- Taking self-destructive actions out of anger or revenge, which ultimately harms oneself or one's own interests.

> **Examples :-**

- ❖ "In a corporate setting, refusing to cooperate with a colleague on a critical project because of a personal disagreement, thereby jeopardising the success of the entire team."

- ❖ "Declining a lucrative business opportunity solely to spite a competitor, without considering the potential benefits and growth it could bring to the company."

"So Long And Thanks For All The Fish"-

> **Meaning** :- Expressing gratitude and bidding farewell.

> **Examples :-**

- ❖ "At the end of a successful project, the team lead said, So long and thanks for all the fish to acknowledge the hard work and contributions of the team members."

❖ "During a farewell gathering for a retiring colleague, the CEO ended the speech with the phrase So long and thanks for all the fish, appreciating the employee's dedication and wishing them well in their future endeavours."

"Idealism Kills Mutual Interests Save Lives"-

➤ Meaning: - Implies that while idealistic pursuits may be well-intentioned, they should be balanced with a pragmatic understanding of the broader interests and needs of others

➤ Examples: -

❖ "Despite safety concerns, the idealism of a team member focused on meeting a deadline at all costs kills mutual interests save lives."

❖ "The idealistic team leader's refusal to consider input from others kills mutual interests save lives by hindering collaboration and compromising project success."